Backyard
Poultry
Keeping

Backyard Poultry Keeping

J. C. Jeremy Hobson

Photographs by Rupert Stephenson

THE CROWOOD PRESS

First published in 2007 by
The Crowood Press Ltd
Ramsbury, Marlborough
Wiltshire SN8 2HR

www.crowood.com

© J C Jeremy Hobson 2007

British Library Cataloguing-in-Publication Data
A catalogue record for this book is available from the British Library.

ISBN 978 1 86126 958 4

Illustration Acknowledgements
All the photographs in this book are courtesy of Rupert Stephenson, poultry photographer (www.rupert-fish.co.uk).

Line illustrations by Keith Field.

Disclaimer
The author and the publisher do not accept any responsibility in any manner whatsoever for any error or omission, nor any loss, damage, injury or liability of any kind incurred as a result of the use of any of the information contained in this book, or reliance upon it.

Typeset by Carreg Limited, Ross-on-Wye, Herefordshire

Printed and bound in Singapore by Craft Print International Ltd

Contents

Introduction

Over 80 per cent of homes in the UK have gardens or outdoor space. They vary from the wild acres of the country mansion to a few yards of terrace in the town, and consist of an assorted conglomeration of lawns, flowerbeds, hedges, yards and plant pots.

Although all are very different in size and content, the majority of outdoor spaces can, with a little ingenuity, forethought and neighbourly consideration, accommodate some form of poultry. The smallest of backyards is big enough to house a trio of tiny bantams such as the Rosecomb or Sebright; an average-sized back garden can be home to a pen of prolific egg-laying large fowl; and in the back paddock of a country property, examples of almost any variety of the poultry world could, quite literally, be on the doorstep.

There are several ways to prevent poultry from damaging a garden and the solutions do not necessarily require the use of unsightly fencing. In the really small garden chickens and bantams with feathered legs are the ideal choice, as these do not, or cannot, scratch up the grass on lawns quite as much as other breeds. Chicken wire may be laid flat on herbaceous borders or annual beds in winter – the plants will grow up through the wire but the birds will be unable to scratch them up. With a little lateral thinking and ingenuity, almost all potential problems associated with keeping poultry in a relatively small area can be negated.

If you have no outside space at all, it may be possible to rent an allotment on which to house your poultry. Some local council rules may specify under approved by-laws that no livestock can be kept on an allotment, but others do allow it. If you are permitted to keep poultry on council-run land, you will be upholding a long-standing tradition – around the time of the Second World War, almost every city allotment in Britain had a corner fenced off as a poultry run.

What exactly is meant by the word 'poultry'? Although when used by Victorian writers such as Richard Jefferies, it evokes a pastoral picture of hens scratching around the farmyard and surrounding fields, in its widest sense it is generally used to describe all of the accepted domestic fowl, such as bantams, chickens, ducks, geese, guinea-fowl and turkeys.

Backyard poultry keeping can be a rewarding hobby, providing pleasure, eggs and meat. The birds are generally cheap to buy and cost little to keep; they demand relatively little space and only a small proportion of their owner's time. The secret of success, however, lies in choosing the right type of bird for the particular situation.

The purpose of this book is to prove that, whatever the size of your backyard, it is possible to indulge in a little of the rural 'good life'; no one should be put off the idea by the thought that their garden is too small.

1

Why, What and Where

With good-quality free-range eggs and organically produced chickens easily available from supermarkets and farmer's markets, the thought of 'growing' your own might seem expensive and time-consuming. Indeed, there are a number of important factors to consider before contemplating the possibility of keeping poultry in your backyard: the need to provide some form of housing and section off a portion of the garden; the cost of buying food and feeding utensils, and the birds themselves; the possibility of disease; and the sometimes extremely difficult task of finding someone willing and able to look after your stock when you are away on holiday or business.

But almost all hobbies are fraught with potential difficulties before the ultimate aim is achieved, so why should any negative thoughts outweigh the advantages when it comes to this particular pastime? And what advantages! A regular daily supply of fresh eggs is the most obvious and, provided that you can bear to kill off your own stock when the time is right, there is the prospect of a meat dish that actually tastes as it should and has not been pumped full of growth hormones in life or water in death. It is, it must be admitted, easy enough to find a decent chicken for Sunday lunch and also a turkey at the right time of year, but it might prove more tricky to find a supplier of geese for a traditional Christmas dinner or half a dozen quail to eat cold with friends at a midsummer picnic?

A beautiful garden and a pen of poultry can, despite what people may tell you, work well together. There are many advantages to combining gardening and poultry keeping, not least the recycling of the readily available supply of excess vegetables and kitchen scraps, which may be fed to poultry and will eventually enhance the nutritional content of the soil via the addition of floor litter to the compost heap. A small combined house and run containing three or four chickens that is regularly moved across the lawn will soon, because of the nitrogen in the bird's droppings, create a green sward that no

A living weathercock set against the backdrop of a flourishing garden: proof, if proof were needed, that poultry and gardens can co-exist.

amount of artificial fertilizers can achieve. Ducks can rid a garden of unwanted slugs. Geese, because of their method of grazing, will nibble out the leaders on individual grass plants, thus encouraging the growth of strong healthy side-shoots as well as virtually eradicating mosses that threaten to smother grass.

However, the biggest advantage and the best reason to bother with poultry must be the fact that, as well as their undoubted practical value, any form of fowl brings a garden or backyard to life. Their colours and characters provide a year-round interest that is far greater than that of even the most exotic of plants. The enthusiastic plantsman or woman already showing their garden produce at the various agricultural shows may even, in time, be tempted to extend their exhibiting activities and begin showing their home-bred poultry.

CONSIDERING THE OPTIONS

As well as the obvious attractions of eggs and meat, there is also the possibility of breeding and selling on stock that is surplus to your own requirements. If this is carried out sensibly and efficiently, you

9

should be able to subsidize your own poultry keeping; you might even be able to make a profit. It is important to be familiar with the types of fowl that will sell and those that will not; it is pointless breeding stock that no one wants and that will eventually take up housing and pens that could be better utilized.

Chickens (and bantams) are, understandably, the most popular type in the world (there are, apparently, at least seven thousand million of them, outnumbering people by three to two). No matter whether the backyard is in Scunthorpe or Seattle, Bodmin or the Bahamas, chickens need only a patch of earth to scratch and a quiet corner in which to lay, and have few specific dietary requirements. In return, they provide eggs for breakfast and meat for dinner.

For the person with a sizeable backyard, a pen of ducks is a feasible option. Provided that the right breed is selected, they will lay a surprising number of eggs, although it must be admitted that, like goose eggs, they are richer than hen's eggs and something of an acquired taste. Ducks have the advantage over chickens of requiring less elaborate housing. As table birds, they are fast growers and a ten-week-old bird may weigh as much as 2.3–2.7kg (5–6lb).

It is commonly thought that ducks and geese require water to swim in, but, while they will be undoubtedly happier with a small pond or bath in which to bathe, all they actually require for their

All ducks and geese really need in the way of water is a fresh, clean supply.

health is fresh drinking water and perhaps a bowl or bucket in which they can dunk their heads to keep their eyes clean and preen themselves. On the down side, they can be a little messy in a really small garden, but even this should not preclude the possibility of a few 'bantam' ducks, many types of which will lay almost as many eggs as their large counterparts.

Geese are hardy, virtually disease-free, easy to look after and make terrific 'guard dogs'. They will fend for themselves as long as the area in which they are kept has plenty of grass and, even in the winter, require nothing more than a simple fox-proof shelter and a few handfuls of grain. Although they are generally kept for their meat and for breeding stock to sell on, they will also lay well during the spring and early summer months. Old birds should not be killed off, as they continue to be fertile to a great age.

Turkeys require housing similar to chickens and, like ducks, are fast growers. They tend not to be as hardy as chickens, however, and need more space than the average small garden permits. Some turkey stags can weigh up to 18kg (40lb); this is too large for the majority of households and a more normal weight to aim for at maturity would be around 7–8kg (16–18lb), especially if you intend to sell to outsiders. The breed is, therefore, obviously an important factor in your choice of stock.

Because of their noisy nature, guinea-fowl are not ideal for the small suburban garden.

The guinea-fowl is not always considered as a backyard bird, but it is useful both as an egg-layer (laying perhaps as many as a hundred in season) and as a table bird. Dressed out, it weighs about 1.6kg ($3^1/_2$ lb) and, being closely related to the pheasant, has a slightly 'gamey' texture and flavour to its meat. On free-range, they will pick up seeds, weeds and insects and require very little extra feeding. They prefer to roost in the trees rather than in a house made available to them and it may be necessary to clip one of their wings to prevent them from wandering on to a neighbour's property. Guinea-fowl are extremely noisy and, like Chinese geese, will screech and call at the slightest disturbance – around a stable yard or quiet secluded country cottage, this may well be a considerable advantage, but would not be very popular in a suburban garden!

Quail are an interesting proposition and many backyard breeders of the past have been tempted into thinking that, because of the quick 'turnover' – seventeen days to incubate, six weeks to mature, egg laying at six weeks, and a bird mature and ready for the table at around nine weeks – they will make their fortune. Unfortunately, they have tended to over-estimate the market. However, they are certainly worth considering as an option for home consumption. They are tiny, so at least two birds per person are required for a meal and there is the chore of several minutes' plucking for a few seconds' eating. They are, however, prolific egg-layers, producing 200 to 300 hundred over a period of ten to twelve months.

Black and Lavender Dutch: examples of 'true' bantams.

WHAT GOES WHERE

Of course, it is not possible to keep a turkey on a terrace or a goose in a gazebo and much depends on the size and layout of the garden or backyard. Generally, however, if you have space for a large rabbit hutch and run, it should be possible to use the same layout for a trio of small bantams. The smallest 'true' bantams are, it must be admitted, more ornamental than practical, but they will, nevertheless, provide a reasonable supply of eggs for breakfast during the spring and summer. With a little more space, it should be possible to choose one of the lighter Mediterranean breeds that will lay well all year round and have the added advantage of being less likely to go broody than some of the heavier types.

Space sufficient for an average-sized dog kennel and run will provide a home for three to six large chickens and an aviary could house several quail or just a few bantams. A garden shed can be put to good use if an outside run is attached or the interior is sectioned off to provide several smaller units. Indeed, it is possible, although not desirable, to keep some smaller varieties of poultry intensively and, in the case of bantams or quail (especially the latter), perhaps even on a 'tier' system where pens are arranged at floor and waist level.

With the exception of quail, which require cages or an aviary-type situation, most other examples of poultry will need a fenced-in garden if they are not to become a nuisance to neighbours. Even so, lighter breeds of chickens and bantams may need to have their wings clipped – the primary feathers are cut on one wing, so as to unbalance the bird in the event of it attempting to fly – or to have pen areas that are netted over.

With the exception of ducks and geese, poultry greatly enjoy dust baths and will enjoy them even more if they have access to flower beds! Lay chicken wire flat on herbaceous borders or annual beds in winter. The plants will grow up through the wire but the birds will be unable to scratch them up. Encourage them to dust elsewhere by

---

True Bantams

A 'true' bantam is one for which there is no large fowl counterpart. Other 'bantam' varieties are those derived from dwarfing or miniaturizing large fowl breeds.

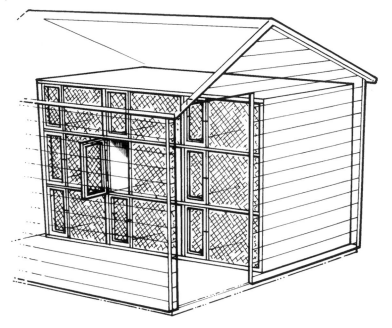

By sectioning the interior of a garden shed into a 'tier' system, it should be possible to house quail or small bantams.

providing a dusting shelter, which only needs to be a covered frame on legs about 60cm (2ft) high. If you dig the soil under this frame and add sand, or even the ashes from a wood fire, they will soon learn to use this rather than your precious flower beds.

If your main intention is to breed bantam ducks, remember that ducks make awful mothers. You will need either to keep a pen of two or three bantam chickens in the hope that, when you want to sit a clutch of duck eggs, at least one of them will be broody, or use an incubator, in which case a small brooding unit will also be required. Have you space for the bantams as well as the ducks? Have you a suitable shed and electricity supply for the incubator and brooder?

Despite all the options available, realistically, the size of property will obviously dictate what types of poultry can be considered and, in the interest of health and hygiene, you should always err on the side of caution when it comes to stocking numbers. Although there may be adequate space for what you have in mind, it is important to ensure that the chosen location is not likely to upset any immediate neighbours: a layout tucked tight against the boundary fence

Unfortunately, few people can aspire to the sort of back garden that is ideally suited to all types of poultry!

may well suit you, but smells or early-morning cock-crowing may offend, and left-over food might encourage vermin such as rats and mice.

THE SMALL GARDEN OR YARD

It is reasonable to assume that a back garden or paved area will be part of a terraced or semi-detached property and, as such, will obviously have neighbours. Some may be in favour of your venture while others may not. Before going any further with your plans, it is essential that you discuss your ideas with them and gauge their opinions. If you go ahead without any form of consultation, you may find yourself subject to complaints and subsequent visitations from your local Environmental Health Authority (*see* 'Avoiding Problems', page 22).

In a small garden or backyard, it should be possible to keep three chickens or six bantams in a house and run measuring approximately 3 x 1m (10 x $3^1/_2$ ft). If the area is grassed, a movable 'fold unit' can be a viable option, provided that it is shifted every day. With some careful planning, the birds need not be on the same piece of grass more than once a week.

15

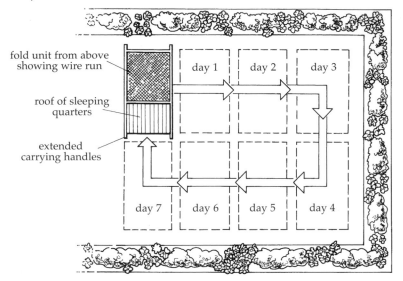

fold unit from above
showing wire run

roof of sleeping
quarters

extended
carrying handles

day 1 | day 2 | day 3

day 7 | day 6 | day 5 | day 4

By creating a regular pattern of moving a fold unit across the lawn on a daily basis, the grass will suffer no ill effects, and the birds will thrive on fresh vegetation and a natural supply of insects.

Assuming that the area can be periodically disinfected, a static house and run could be the best option if the backyard is literally a yard, and consists of concrete or paving slabs. In this instance, it would be best to have the roof of the house continuing the full length of the run and also to enclose the back and sides, leaving only

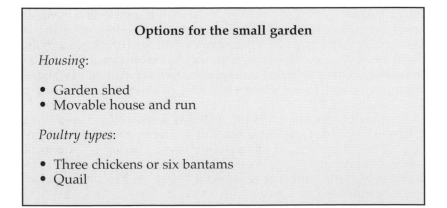

Options for the small garden

Housing:

- Garden shed
- Movable house and run

Poultry types:

- Three chickens or six bantams
- Quail

the wire-netting front portion open to the elements. By doing this, it should be possible to include a base of fine gravel, sand or wood bark, which will provide both scratching and dusting material and can be periodically taken out and sieved in order to remove faeces, vegetable stalks and discarded feathers.

THE MIDDLE-SIZED GARDEN

Apparently, according to recently published statistics, the average or middle-sized British back garden is around 1,036sq m (3,400sq ft), large enough, according to the Turkey Club UK, to accommodate a pair of turkeys. (At one time, turkeys were regularly reared in small gardens by cottagers who would keep just one or two hens. One visit to the male bird would be sufficient to fertilize an entire batch of eggs and therefore ensure a few birds for the table in the winter months.)

Such a garden will also provide a home for any one of the following options:

- a couple of geese;
- a small pen of ornamental ducks;
- two or three movable arks and runs, each of which could contain a trio or quartet of bantams; or
- a permanent shed and run built to house a flock of perhaps a dozen hens.

Inevitably, the accommodation possible in the average middle-sized garden will depend on its shape. A long, narrow garden is perhaps best for such a project as, provided it does not back directly on to a neighbour's house, a poultry 'unit' can be sited discreetly at the end of the garden.

If birds have to be penned and there is a worry that the area might become a quagmire in wet winter weather, it might be worth considering an adaptation of what has become known as the Balfour Method. In this method, a hen house is placed in the centre of a deep-litter yard, from which a couple of runs run on to grass. In an average-sized garden, it may be possible to have the house on a fenced concrete or pea-shingle base. Two adjoining pens could cover a grassed area on to which birds can run in good weather, but from which they are excluded in bad. Having two pens allows them to be used on alternate days, lessening general wear and tear. It is not dissimilar to the idea proposed for the larger gardens (*see* page 19).

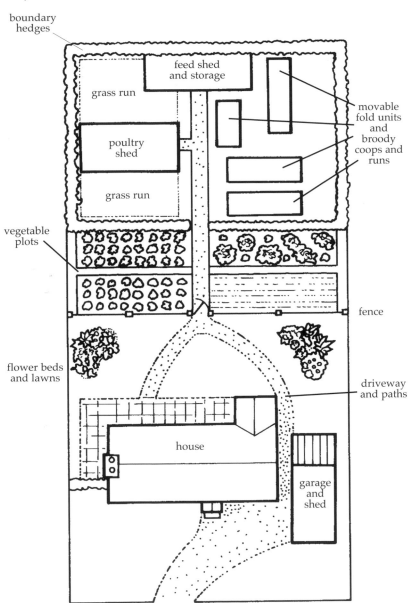

The ideal plan for the backyard poultry keeper.

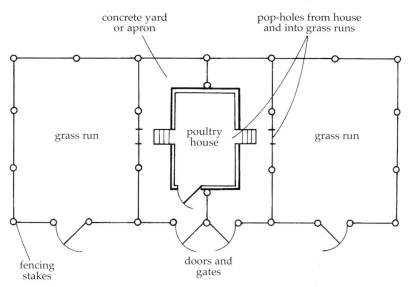

concrete yard
or apron

pop-holes from house
and into grass runs

grass run

poultry
house

grass run

fencing
stakes

doors and
gates

Loosely based on the Balfour system, a static shed should have two runs leading from it so that each can be 'rested' on a regular basis.

A middle-sized or 'average' garden can accommodate a few call or bantam ducks.

Options for the middle-sized garden

Housing:

- Garden shed
- Movable house and run
- Static house with permanent run (plus occasional access to garden)

Poultry types:

- Chickens and/or bantams
- Small pen of bantam or light ducks
- Quail
- Two turkeys
- Pair or trio of call-ducks

THE LARGE GARDEN

With a large secluded garden at your disposal, there is, within reason, no limit to the type of poultry you can keep. Your only restrictions may be how much space you wish to utilize and how much time you have to ensure that your birds are kept healthy and are correctly managed. Larger properties, especially those in rural areas, are quite likely to include at least one out-building and these can quite often be adapted into some superb poultry housing. An open-fronted shed, for example, only requires the exposed part to be fitted with secure wire netting panels and the floor given a thick base of suitable litter for it to become an ideal building in which to fatten table birds or to breed turkeys.

Large gardens with no buildings and no nearby neighbours can provide a home for guinea-fowl where, as long as there are trees in which they can take shelter from the unwanted attentions of a fox, they will be quite happy. Guinea-fowl also have the advantage of being able to have almost total free-range without the keen gardener worrying for his crops – they are more interested in a diet of seeds, bugs and insects than in what might be growing in the vegetable patch.

Geese also make a wonderful addition to the larger property, especially when kept in a shrubbery, grass paddocks or a mini-

Geese make a wonderful addition to the larger backyard. (Note the 'dewlap' on the throat, which can be prominent in some breeds and almost non-existent in others.)

Options for the large garden

Housing:

- Static buildings equipped with dual runs
- Several movable coops and runs for breeding and hatching purposes
- Shed for housing exhibition stock or for storage and preparation of poultry-related produce
- Small pond

Poultry types:

- Chickens/bantams
- Ducks/geese
- Quail
- Turkeys

---

orchard where they will keep the grass at bowling-green level. Even though they do not need it for their health's sake, geese will require some protection from foxes or wandering dogs.

AVOIDING PROBLEMS

The whole point behind the title of this book is to make the would-be enthusiast realize that, in nine cases out of ten, it is possible to indulge in poultry keeping at one level or another. It is, however, fair to say that some urban gardens are less suitable than rural ones: there are more people living closer together; most properties have extremely small gardens; and some fellow residents have a NIMBY ('Not in my back yard') attitude, quite literally in this case.

By following certain guidelines you can avoid many potential problems, but before you even consider backyard poultry keeping, you must check your property title deeds for any restrictive covenants, and maybe consult the local council in order to ascertain whether any by-laws totally forbid the keeping of any form of live-stock. There are also laws appertaining to the keeping of certain numbers of laying hens for egg consumption or breeding. In addition, if you are lucky enough to have more space, and want to build up a flock of over fifty birds, you will need to register them with DEFRA.

It is a complicated subject, but it might be worth mentioning the following facts, which could help in avoiding potential problems. An area of ground of more than an acre might technically be classi-fied as a smallholding and, if you are intending to sell your poultry produce on a semi-commercial basis, you may need to officially reg-ister the land as such. If you have bought or are renting a house with agricultural ties or which has previously been registered as a small-holding, you should ensure that you know the smallholding num-ber. Agricultural property of all sizes comes under the Agricultural Holdings Act and, as such, is under the care of your local DEFRA offices. Give them a ring to clarify your own particular situation: if the property has always been a smallholding it will certainly already have been issued with a number; if not, you may have to register or re-register. The good news is that doing so costs you nothing; the bad news is that what you can eventually do on your piece of land depends entirely on the views of your planning department as to what buildings they will allow you to construct!

Generally, however, the most important factors to consider are the location of poultry housing in relation to other residences, the

If they are not kept under control, rats will soon make a home around the poultry sheds, and rat runs, such as these tunnels under the concrete base, will become obvious.

storage of feed to avoid rodent problems, the prompt and proper disposal of litter and waste matter and, obviously, the health and well-being of the birds themselves. It is essential that the birds are given adequate space, proper nutrition, sufficient attention and protection from the environment and predators.

The appearance of all types of equipment and housing, particularly external runs, should not detract from the overall appearance of the surroundings. Exteriors of sheds and other structures should be kept painted and well maintained. Proper landscaping can provide screening and also help muffle sounds. All types of poultry have their own characteristic noises and smells. You should house them in such a way that the odour is not offensive and any noise is no louder than the normal speaking voice of an adult human. This can be done by insulating quarters, providing adequate ventilation and using good sanitation practices.

The backyard poultry keeper must make every effort not to infringe on his neighbour, who may be sensitive to noise, odour, flies, rodents and unsightliness due to inadequately designed and maintained facilities. People differ in their tolerance to the same conditions and, just because one neighbour may not object, it does not necessarily follow that another will share your enthusiasm for the hobby.

If you discover that, despite having made all the right approaches regarding neighbours and the authorities, and finding that they are initially keen on your ideas, neighbours begin to object when you put your plans into practice, you must act promptly to solve the problem.

It is far better to take preventive steps from the outset rather than wait until any complaints are officially registered. If it does go wrong, you may be legally forced to get rid of your stock, and if you fail to do so you are quite likely to be prosecuted. Likewise, the owners of a loudly crowing cockerel could find themselves subject to a noise abatement order. Remember that you do not need to keep a cock bird with your flock unless you intend to breed from it and it would be absolute folly even to contemplate the prospect of rearing surplus male birds for the table with being aware of the fact that, as they mature, they become increasingly vocal. It would be possible to avoid this happening by caponizing young cockerels, but such a practice is unlikely to be a viable option for the small-time backyarder. If meat production is your aim, it is far better to purchase female birds bred specifically for the table. It is also important to be aware that even hens will cackle at certain times of the day, especially when they have just laid or have been disturbed by a sudden noise or unfamiliar human or animal.

Remember that it is not essential to keep a cock bird with your flock unless you intend breeding.

2

Making Choices

Having considered the options available and the reasons why you wish to keep a certain type of bird, the next question to be addressed relates to breeds. A pure-bred has certain advantages, as does a cross-breed. Many poultry keepers claim that the latter have several serious advantages over the former as they are generally less inter-bred and therefore more vigorous and healthy. Indeed, some crosses have become so well known throughout the years that they are almost accepted as being a true breed.

There are many examples of suitable crosses. The Embden/Toulouse cross of geese is popular because of its dual-purpose function of producing a good supply of eggs and a heavy carcass; in the pure-bred form, however, poultry keepers would probably choose the Embden for egg-laying and the Toulouse for meat.

The Embden goose has always been popular for its egg-laying potential.

The Light Sussex/Rhode Island Red cross has always been popular. Along with certain other breeds of chicken, such as the Brown Leghorn and Barred Rock, they present the keeper with the advantage of being able to sex any resultant chicks at day-old. Therefore, if only egg-layers are required, the male chicks can be immediately culled, avoiding the expense and time of keeping them until an age at which they can be sexed by the more obvious methods of differing plumage and a heavier comb.

Sex-Linking

The most common sex-linkage is between 'gold' cocks and 'silver' hens. A Rhode Island Red cock mated with a Light Sussex hen will produce brown or 'gold' pullet chicks and creamy-white or 'silver' cockerel chicks.

OBTAINING STOCK

Auctions

Beware of buying stock at an auction: it is too easy to be carried away in the heat of the moment and to buy birds that are, to use jargon currently in vogue at the moment, 'not fit for purpose'. It is also easy to let your heart rule your head and pay more than the birds are worth. Another downside to this type of purchase is the fact that it is impossible to handle stock and check them out health-wise. If, for whatever reason, it is thought a good idea to buy at auction (and to be fair, many local poultry clubs do hold spring and autumn sales at which some excellent stock can be purchased), be sure to take someone experienced with you. It is easy to make a mistake with something as fundamental as sexing, especially with geese or guinea-fowl.

Private Sources

Unless you have got to know the person with stock to sell as a result of meeting them at shows or poultry clubs, exercise caution when responding to newspaper adverts or when following up contacts via a third person; you know the sort of thing: 'Oh yes, a mate of

Wherever possible, it pays to buy your stock from someone whose birds have had considerable success on the show bench.

mine has just what you're looking for. Go and see him and tell him I sent you. He'll see you right.' Nine times out of ten, he will, but once again there is no harm taking someone along with you whose opinion you can really trust. If the would-be vendor is an honest type (and most involved in the poultry world are), he will certainly have no objection to someone offering a second opinion. Watch out for genuine enthusiasts who are new to the game and may be selling off stock surplus to requirements – if they do not know what they are selling, you could come away either with rubbish or their best birds!

Arguably, the best way of buying is from private breeders who advertise regularly in reputable magazines such as *Fancy Fowl*, especially those who have gained a considerable reputation on the show bench and have therefore much to lose by selling poor stock.

Selling Classes

Many shows and exhibitions include a selling class and these are likely to be full of good-quality birds from the same sources as above. These events are advertised in reputable magazines such as *Fancy Fowl*, *Smallholder* and *Country Smallholding*.

When to Buy

Do not leave buying breeding stock until spring. Poultry fanciers prefer to dispose of surplus birds in the autumn in order to cut down on the costs involved with over-wintering and the problems associated with too many birds on wet ground during bad weather. It therefore makes sense to buy them in the autumn, when prices are cheaper and there is likely to be more of choice. Also, if you leave purchasing birds until the spring, much of the early breeding opportunities will be missed while waiting for new birds to settle in and for fresh males to mate and eggs to become fertile.

CHOOSING THE RIGHT BIRDS

Choosing stock is a matter of common sense: all stock should be bright-eyed with a clean back end and no mucus coming from the nostrils or beak. The combs and wattles should, where appropriate,

A good example of a healthy turkey stag.

be waxy in texture. Most combs ought to be red, but there are exceptions: a Silkie, for example, has a purple-coloured comb. Wattles in other breeds can be either white or red. Turkeys are, however, a law until themselves and the head-piece of an adult stag may vary in colour from bright red to ice-blue (and extend or contract!), depending on whether or not he is displaying at the time.

No matter what the type, a healthy bird should be an integral part of the flock, not moping and isolated in a corner. Over a period of time, it will be observed moving from food and water and foraging. Healthy free-range chickens, bantams, turkeys and guinea-fowl will spend some time either dust-bathing or just resting in the sunshine and even intensively reared quail enjoy a 'dust' bath in clean shavings. Given an adequate supply of water, ducks and geese carry out their equivalent of a dust bath by splashing and cleaning themselves.

The great advantage of buying from a private vendor is that you can actually handle birds in order to see at close quarters whether or not they are healthy specimens. It is important to do this correctly.

Healthy birds should spend a good portion of their day dust-bathing.

Generally, poultry should be held close to your body, with one hand being passed under the bird's body in order to hold the legs securely tight; the other hand should offer support and a gentle restraint to the exposed wing. In the case of waterfowl, however, the legs must *not* be held tightly together because their hip joints are set at the side rather than in the middle and you could cause damage.

When examining any type of poultry, check that the leg joints are normal and not swollen, that there is a reasonable amount of flesh around the breast-bone or keel, and that the feet are not deformed. The eyes must be bright and free from any pale cast impeding vision; the beak should be straight, with both the upper and lower mandibles able to connect.

Finally, look at the overall condition of the bird. It should be free from parasites and lice. Check for scaly-leg mite in all types of poultry (with the exception of waterfowl, which do not seem to succumb to this particular problem). The feather condition should be tight and glossy: a condition that is most often seen in birds that have been given total free-range and the chance to become weather-hardened.

The head of a Buff Orpington, showing bright eyes, a clean comb and a well-formed beak – all essential attributes of a good and healthy bird.

If you are buying laying chickens, it is possible to check whether they are pullets or mature hens by feeling the distance between the two sharp bones on either side of the vent. If you can fit only one finger between these bones, in all probability the bird is not yet laying. A hen 'in lay' will also have a large, moist vent whereas one that is not will have a small, dry vent.

KEEPING MALE BIRDS

Many people believe that a male bird is needed in order for females to lay, or to watch over them, but this is untrue. In the absence of a male, females will find their own pecking order or hierarchy, with one of the more dominant birds taking on the male's role. Obviously, if you intend to breed from your stock then it is essential that at least one male forms part of the flock, but, in all other situations, you should consider the disadvantages carefully before choosing to keep a male bird. Generally, a male bird will eat a lot of food but lay no eggs and, more seriously, your birds may be more stressed by the unwanted attentions of a male than they would if left to their own devices. This is particularly true in the case of some duck breeds; often, the drake's idea of courtship is nothing less than rape. A cockerel may disturb your neighbours with his crowing, and his spurs and claws can damage the hen's backs with his repeated mating attempts.

Some breeds of poultry are known to be more aggressive than others, so if you decide to keep any of these it will pay not to include a male unless absolutely necessary. You should also be aware of the possibility of attacks on children; a bantam cock attacking the back of the legs can be frightening enough for an adult, but really terrifying for a small child. Likewise, a gander (and, indeed, a goose) can inflict a nasty nip.

If a male is required for breeding purposes, then perhaps the best way of ensuring that the females suffer the least damage from his attentions is to have sufficient in the flock so that he has no option but to divide his attentions between them all rather than concentrating on just a few. (*See* Chapter 6 for the best ratio of males to females in a breeding pen.)

It is the opinion of most poultry fanciers that the male is the most important member of the breeding pen and this fact should be remembered when making your eventual choice. If his background is doubtful, many of his faults will be transferred to his offspring. He must come from quality breeding stock if he is to have any hope of producing good progeny.

CHOOSING BREEDS

Chickens and Bantams

Should the production of eggs just be a bonus to having some poultry in the garden, then the type of breed chosen is perhaps less important than the colour or shape. Silkies, for example, are extremely attractive birds, excellent as children's pets and unusual in their feathering, but they will often produce not much more than a clutch of eggs before going broody.

But even chicken breeds need selecting with care. A light Mediterranean breed will lay countless eggs but will never produce a meat carcass. If they are to be allowed access to the garden, even more care may be required in their selection as some, notably the Sumatra and White-faced Spanish, are the absolute devils for scratching, while furry-footed Cochins, Pekins and Brahmas do far less damage.

If eggs are the primary requirement, it is important to choose one of the known egg-laying breeds. Rhode Island Reds and Sussex are noted as pure breeds that lay extremely well (around 260 eggs per

Brahmas cause less damage to the garden than some other breeds.

year) even though they are traditionally classed as a dual-purpose (in other words, egg-layer and table) bird. Most hybrids will match, or probably exceed, that number, but have a shorter laying 'lifespan'. If you want to sell the eggs, it will pay to choose a breed that lays a coloured egg. Although there is no difference in nutritional value between eggs with a white or chocolatey-brown shell, it is a proven fact that a tray of the latter will sell before the former. The Maran, Welsummer and Barnevelder breeds all produce a dark brown egg and are popular breeds purely because of this. The Araucana is of particular interest because of its unusually coloured blue egg, while other breeds lay white, cream, tinted, speckled, olive and even plum-coloured eggs.

Skin colour is one of the most important characteristics of a table chicken. Until fairly recently, white-skinned varieties were preferred in the UK whereas a yellow skin was favoured in the USA and elsewhere. Nowadays, with the desire for an organic-looking, corn-fed bird, the yellow-skinned types are increasingly finding favour in the UK as well.

A real table bird is one that comes from a breed that is well known for its good qualities – in other words, one that carries the

A winning plate of coloured eggs.

maximum of breast meat. The rearer has a choice of possible breeds and will need to decide whether to go ahead with the purchase of a commercially produced bird such as the Ross Cobb, or stick with one of the more traditional meat-producing breeds such as the Dorking, Indian Game, Bresse and Sussex. All of these undoubtedly possess a good food/meat conversion ratio, but will take more weeks to reach maturity and a good killing weight.

Geese

The domestic goose of Europe is the descendant of the migratory Greylag, from which it differs only in its increased size. Although domesticated since the time of the Romans, it has not been subject to much variation over the ensuing generations. Compared with other forms of livestock, geese are not very efficient at converting

Chinese are an unusual and very attractive breed, but can be quite noisy.

grass into meat, but they are excellent grazers of rough areas, as well as being cheap to keep and an interesting option for the backyard poultry keeper with a larger garden.

After the Crimean War, a Russian variety of goose was introduced into the UK and this breed, now commonly known as the Sebastopol, does differ slightly in that its feathers are singularly elongated and sometimes even curled and twisted. It is smaller than the normal goose and is usually kept as an exhibition or 'fancy' breed rather than for any practical use.

Another interesting and very attractive breed is the Chinese, sometimes known as the Knob-fronted or Swan goose. Although perfectly distinct as a species, having a different number of vertebrae in its neck, it breeds quite freely with all other types of geese and the hybrids produced are fertile. Known in the USA as the African goose, it has been crossed with Embden and Toulouse varieties and the produce of this cross is considered to be extremely fertile and profitable. The Chinese has a loud 'clanging' call, which makes it popular as a watchdog in quiet secluded places, but less so when there are neighbours to consider.

Heavy breeds of domestic geese that are popular as table birds include the Embden and Toulouse; medium varieties include the American Buff, Brecon Buff, Buff Back, Grey Back and West of England; and one of the best-known lighter egg-laying types is the Roman. The Chinese and Sebastopol are considered good layers by some fanciers.

Categorization

Like chickens and bantams, waterfowl are categorized according to their 'weight' and geese are divided into 'light', 'medium' and 'heavy'. Ducks are slightly different in that they are known as 'bantam', 'light' or 'heavy'.

Ducks

All breeds of duck, apart from the Muscovy, are thought to have descended from the common Mallard or wild duck. The Muscovy, although a domestic breed, was introduced into the UK from South America in the mid-seventeenth century and there is doubt in some quarters as to whether it is really a duck or goose! Either way, it is

A Muscovy duck – in my opinion, a breed to be avoided at all cost!

greedy, messy and certainly not the most attractive of birds; apart from its possible use as a table bird (and there are better alternatives), it is best ignored by the backyard poultry keeper. The drake will mate with the common duck but the resultant hybrids are sterile.

Of the early table ducks, the Aylesbury had no equal and in the nineteenth century almost all white ducks were known by that name, because the best came from the Vale of Aylesbury. What is known as an Aylesbury today has, over the years, most likely had hybrid broiler and Pekin blood introduced into its make-up.

There are several well-established domestic breeds, all with known characteristics and performances, and the choice of breed depends only on whether the production of eggs or meat is the main aim. Even the average-sized garden could accommodate a few call ducks, which lay surprisingly well and make very little mess.

The showing of ducks is an increasingly popular pastime. If you are intending to exhibit your birds, make sure that you visit a few shows before making a final choice of breed.

The most common 'heavy' or table breeds of duck are the Aylesbury, Blue Swedish, Cayuga, Muscovy, Pekin, Rouen, Saxony and Silver Appleyard. Included in the 'light' or egg-laying section are the Abacot Ranger, Buff Orpington, Crested White, Indian Runner (*see* below), Khaki Campbell and Welsh Harlequin. Black East Indian, the many varieties of call duck, Miniature Crested, Miniature Silver Appleyard and Silver are all 'bantam' types.

Indian Runner

The Indian Runner used to be known as the 'Penguin Duck', as a result of its original colouring and erect stature. It is popular in Britain due to it being a hardy forager and a good layer and was first introduced into Dumfriesshire by a ship's captain returning from Malaya in 1876.

Turkeys

The most economical way of buying in turkeys is at day-old but they will of course need some sort of heating. For the Christmas market, the optimum time to take delivery is the beginning of July: older birds that do not require brooding can usually be sourced at a later date than this, but they will cost more, depending on their age. Table birds are best bought in this way too.

Turkey breeding has been largely dominated by the magnificent American bronze breed, which was derived from wild stock and domesticated by the Aztecs in Mexico. They were taken to Spain in 1500 and introduced from there to England in 1524. The first turkeys to be bred in Britain would have been bronze like their wild ancestors, but by 1860 the main colour was black. As East Anglia was the main breeding region, they soon became known as Norfolk Blacks. The Norfolk Black and the Cambridge Bronze are therefore thought to have been the first British turkey breeds and have, over the years, been crossed to create the Norfolk Bronze. At one time, white turkeys were known as either the White Austrian or the White Holland; however, it was the small American Beltsville that has had the most influence on the breeding of the modern white bird.

Old-fashioned farmyard turkeys take about ten weeks longer than their modern counterparts to mature, so if it is intended to keep turkeys purely as table birds it is worth remembering that the

Table birds – in this instance, broilers – are most economically reared from day-old.

commercial broad-breasted intensive breeds will mature more quickly than some of the single-breasted older types of bird. Traditional breeds will, however, command a better price, both as stock birds and as a carcass.

Traditional breeds also have the advantage of being able to mate successfully, unlike the highly bred, broad-breasted whites of the commercial turkey world, some of which can only reproduce by means of artificial insemination.

As free-range birds, adult turkeys are quite hardy but young birds are particularly sensitive to damp so they will need a fair amount of care and attention during the early part of their life. Once the poults have 'shot the red' – the stage at which the red skin of the neck shines through the moulting chick feathers – they are as weatherproof as their parents.

The Norfolk Bronze and the White are probably the best known of turkey varieties, but other high-breasted historical standard breeds include the Bourbon Red, Buff, Blue (Lavender), Narragansett, Nebraskan, Pied (Crollwitzer), Royal Palm and Spanish Black.

A Norfolk turkey hen.

Guinea-Fowl

Guinea-fowl are obviously not the best choice for a suburban garden but they can quite easily be kept in any reasonably dry locality, provided that it has a few trees in which to roost. They can be quite noisy and are therefore not best suited to small suburban gardens where neighbours may well find them a problem.

Guinea-fowl have always been popular in Europe, especially in France, where some fifty-four million are produced annually for the table market. French birds are slightly heavier than those reared in the UK and are quicker to mature, and some British producers import breeding stock from France in order to benefit from these factors.

Left to her own devices, the guinea hen would, like most birds, lay a clutch of eggs and then go broody. However, if the eggs are removed, it is not unreasonable to expect a hen to continue laying until she has produced as many as 50 to 100 eggs. This means that, as well as keeping guinea-fowl purely as a hobby, egg production and meat are quite a practical option. Take care when removing the eggs from the nest: always do it when you know that the bird is not around to see you and, in an exception to the general rule of poultry keeping, never remove them all. If you do, the hen will find somewhere else to lay and it may take you days of careful watching to find the new location.

Unlike other types of poultry, which have separate breeds, guinea-fowl merely have differing colours. Apart from the normal coloured plumage – grey on the neck with white spotted black feathers on the body – guinea-fowl can be found in about two dozen different colours ranging from chocolate and pewter to purple and lavender. Some specific colours are given names, including White, Lavender, Buff Dundottes and Royal Blue.

Quail

At one time quail could be found wild in certain parts of the English countryside, especially in the eastern counties, but such a sighting

Although there are no specific breeds of guinea-fowl, they are seen in several colours.

today would, unfortunately, be a rare event. In the wild they would lay only two or three clutches a year, each containing ten or twelve eggs, but, given the right indoor conditions, they can be induced to lay continually for the best part of the year and one bird may produce over 200 eggs. They also mature quickly and make good eating and require very little in the way of space. All of these factors make them a serious proposition for the backyard poultry keeper with only a tiny area at his disposal.

Although there are several varieties of quail, the type commonly used in meat and egg production is the Japanese, which also has a vast array of 'local' names, including the Pharaoh and Bible quail. Like guinea-fowl, some true colours are given names: Fawn, Manchurian Golden and Dark-eyed White. One different kind of quail is the larger Bobwhite, which is also occasionally bred for its meat-producing qualities. As might be expected, its eggs are larger than those of the Japanese, but it is, unfortunately, not nearly so prolific.

The Japanese quail (left) is much smaller than its cousin, the Bobwhite, but lays more eggs.

—— 3 ——

Costs, Budgets and Records

Some of the more common commercial poultry hybrids can be quite easily and cheaply purchased and all will thrive in the backyard environments described here. Obviously, rare or pure-breeds could be more difficult to source (*see* 'Obtaining Stock', Chapter 2) and will usually cost more to buy, but keeping them will give you the definite added pleasure of ensuring the continuing survival of a less well-known variety of fowl.

If you are intending to breed on a semi-commercial basis, or at least hope to make your hobby self-financing, some hard-headed business decisions need to be taken. Setting up can be expensive, especially if only a few birds are to be produced and reared. The costings are inevitably high when taking into account capital equipment (*see* page 49). Selling birds can be quite expensive too. There is the cost of advertising to consider; if they are to be sold at auction, there is an entry fee and a percentage to be taken by the auctioneer for his trouble. If prices are poor at the time of selling, it is quite easy to make a loss rather than a profit.

It is a very different matter if poultry is kept in the backyard purely as a hobby, but, even so, it pays to buy the best and make sure that your initial stock are sound, good examples of their breed, free from physical defect and not inbred.

PURCHASING FOWL

Sales and auctions might seem at first to be ideal places from which to source birds due to the variety likely to be on display, but there is a very real danger that your heart will conquer your head and you will come away with something you did not intend to buy. Generally, it is a safer bet to buy from a reputable private vendor (*see* 'Obtaining Stock', Chapter 2).

Prices of stock will vary depending on whether hybrids or pure-breds are chosen; the latter are usually more expensive. If you are looking for chickens, ex-intensive layers, which are kept only for their first laying season and yet have many more years of egg-laying capabilities, are virtually given away and would be a cheap option if eggs are all that is required. Obviously, 'point-of-lay' stock will cost more than youngsters that then need bringing on, but this has to be balanced against the extra time and food required to raise the younger birds to maturity.

The cost of a breeding trio of birds could, depending on the type of poultry that you are after, range from a few pounds to well over £100. At a rare-breeds auction in 2007, bidding was fierce for Buff Orpingtons – a breeding trio sold for £155 and a trio of pullets for £85. A trio of Copper Maran pullets sold for £78, a Silver Cuckoo for £54, and a trio of Old English Game pheasant fowl for £62. Ducks and geese were selling from £15 up to £60 or £70.

Expect to pay an average of somewhere between £25 and £50 for a trio of bantams, and £40 to £70 for the same number of large fowl (with youngsters costing anywhere between £10 and £20 each). A pair of pure-bred but otherwise 'ordinary' ducks might be around £20 or £30 and a pair of breeding geese will set you back anywhere

Some breeds, such as these superb-looking Buff Orpingtons, can be quite expensive to purchase.

between £30 and £40. Adult breeding quail can be bought for £4 or £5 each whilst guinea-fowl are currently available for around £8 to £10 each.

Turkeys and table birds such as the famous French breeds Bresse and Sassos are normally sold either at day-old or just off heat. Fifty day-old turkeys will cost about £200 while the same quantity of good-quality day-old table chickens will be between £75 and £100. This might seem quite expensive when compared with the price of a frozen chicken in the supermarket, but you have the advantage of knowing the provenance of your birds once they reach the killing stage.

HOUSING

General Housing

Chickens, bantams and turkeys may need the most elaborate (and therefore more expensive) housing, while ducks and geese require only a shelter from the weather, dogs and foxes. Guinea-fowl require none at all, as they are quite happy roosting in any available trees, although you do need to ensure that they will not fly off the roost straight into a neighbour's garden and begin dusting in a carefully nurtured vegetable patch.

Always buy the biggest house that your budget will allow and remember that you may have to take the advice of some suppliers with a pinch of salt. They may tell you that a shelter is suitable for a certain number of birds when, realistically, you would be better off reducing their stocking suggestions by as much as half. This is not always the case, however, and you should be able to find a knowledgeable and reputable shed manufacturer.

If a shed seems too cheap, that is probably because it is poorly made and will need replacing in three or four years' time. One that is initially much more expensive should last, almost literally, a lifetime, provided that it is kept off the ground, regularly weatherproofed and has any minor repairs carried out before they become major.

Auxiliary Housing

If you hope to show your stock, you will need some auxiliary housing for use as penning sheds in order to 'train' birds to show to their best advantage. The shed needs to be large enough to hold a bench,

Always buy the biggest poultry house that your budget will allow.

on which there should be space for a couple of show pens. The shed can be multiple use, also accommodating feed bins, carrying boxes and assorted poultry paraphernalia. It must not, however, be allowed to become a dumping ground, as this will attract vermin. A small garden shed will do the job, provided that it is light enough, tall enough for you to stand comfortably and has adequate ventilation.

Those with a large enough backyard to consider selling eggs and meat may have to include hygienic preparation areas to comply with government and local authority regulations.

For more on housing, *see* Chapter 4.

FEEDSTUFFS

The best food might not necessarily be the most expensive and it is more important to ensure that feedstuffs contain the entire requirements essential for the well-being of your birds than it is to consider prices. It might be a cliché, but it is nevertheless true that you will only get out of your poultry what you put in to them.

Having said that, a very cheap product is probably only sold at that price because an important nutritional element has been omitted and replaced with a less expensive alternative. It may also have been poorly produced. On reaching the bottom of a cheap sack of pellets, for example, you often find that a great deal of unwanted and unusable 'dust' remains; no matter how cheap the bag was initially, there is obviously no point in paying for contents that have to be thrown away.

Always seek advice from an experienced backyard poultry keeper as to the best brands of chick crumbs, breeders, layers, waterfowl pellets and suchlike currently on the market.

EQUIPMENT

However seriously you intend to take the business of backyard poultry keeping, there is always the subject of general equipment to consider. Drinkers and feeders are obvious essentials, but money might also need to be invested in incubators, plucking machines and so on.

You can buy a fairly decent 2.5-litre plastic drinker for £10, but a galvanized one will cost three times that amount. A galvanized 9-litre one will be around £40, whereas a plastic one of the same capacity can be had for £12. Eventually a metal one will rust, but only after several years: drop a hard plastic one on to concrete after it has had a winter out in the cold and frost and there is a good chance that it may split. You need to decide whether it is better to spend £40 and hope that your investment will be good for twenty years or to buy cheaply and replace as and when necessary. One option is a system of automatic drinkers (it is possible to buy ones specifically for ducks, which they cannot dirty, get in or upset). If you decide to go for this, you will need to budget not only for the cost of the drinker itself, but also for the additional expenditure involved with plastic piping and header tanks.

An incubator for ten eggs will set you back around £100. Some companies sell larger incubators and brooders together, and you should expect to pay £250 to £350 for these. Brooders on their own are not all that expensive and, if you were only hatching a few chicks, a heat lamp would suffice and cost £15–£20.

It is always possible to shop around and buy specific items cheaper than those quoted, and you can also give some serious thought to the idea of buying second-hand equipment in an effort to save money. There are some good bargains to be had as a result of

Drinkers and feeders are obvious essentials, but is it cheaper in the long run to buy plastic or galvanized?

It is sometimes possible to buy good second-hand equipment, such as incubators, at auctions or farm sales.

scouring the classified ads in local papers, attending farm auctions or asking around fellow members of your local poultry club. Always disinfect and otherwise thoroughly clean any items of dirty second-hand equipment as soon as you get them home, and certainly before using them for the first time.

OFF-SETTING COSTS

By selling eggs, table birds, breeding stock, adults and chicks, the backyard poultry keeper might be able to make his hobby self-financing. For advice on the practicalities of producing and selling eggs and meat, *see* Chapter 8.

There are a couple of additional ways that might help in off-setting costs.

Poultry manure is high in nitrogen, which keeps foliage green and makes an excellent lawn feed when diluted with water.

However, as it is high in ammonia, it will burn plants if applied directly to beds so, before offering it for sale, keep in a heap until it is suitably rotted. The drier the manure, the less it will smell, which is an important point in the backyard, especially one that is in close proximity of neighbours. It would not be a good move if your venture got, quite literally, up their noses!

There may even be a market for good-quality assorted feathers; white-coloured ones will achieve the best prices. After plucking, sort out the feathers, discarding those from the wing or tail, and store them in sacks to dry. If the feathers are soiled, wash them in a bag in a warm solution of wool detergent diluted in rainwater. Either tumble dry or hang the bag outdoors on a bright windy day, shaking and turning it every now and then.

KEEPING FINANCIAL RECORDS

In order to keep track of exactly what your hobby or small business is costing, it is essential to keep *accurate* records every time a purchase is made or a deal is done. This need not be an elaborate or time-consuming exercise and a small book will be sufficient. If you want to use a computer, simply open up a backyard poultry-keeping file and store all the information in there. As well as readily available information on the day-to-day income and expenditure, it will provide fascinating reading in years to come and also be an effective means of comparing costs.

Make a list of appropriate headings such as cost of feed, purchase of birds and medication. If you want to do the thing really well, break down the initial purchase costs of items such as housing, wire netting and feeders as 'capital' expenditure, and off-set them over a period of several years; the exact amount of time depends on the item's likely 'life-span' and the number of years it will serve before it will need to be replaced. For example, if a small ark and run costs £200 to buy, you could reckon on it costing you £40 each year for five years and include that figure in your accounts over the same period rather than costing the whole amount into your first season's records. (As long as it is properly maintained, of course, it should last much longer than five years.)

Although it is easy to factor in the costs of obvious items, it is also important to include the less obvious ones if you are to have any hope of getting a realistic picture of your income and expenditure. These might include rental on a piece of land adjoining your own backyard; lighting to ensure that laying birds have sufficient 'daylight' during the dark winter months; a couple of bottles of whisky at Christmas to the kind greengrocer who lets you have his 'past-their-best' greens throughout the year; membership of your local poultry society; and even the few pence that a dozen leg rings may cost to purchase. Each of these items on its own matters little financially, but, added together over a period of time, they all add to the overall costs.

On the income side, it is equally important to include everything. The glory of being placed among the top three cards at a show is undoubtedly more important than the miniscule amount of prize money you are likely to win as a result, but it is essential that it is included as part of your figures so that it can be compared against money laid out in entry costs and petrol used driving to the show.

Every month, enter the details for income and expenditure beneath the relevant headings and add them all up. If you really want to, you can carry forward the figures at the bottom of the two columns into the following month. This will make your final 'audit' at the end of the year a very simple matter indeed.

It is perhaps too much to suggest that you should have a separate bank account for your poultry-keeping interests – it is, at this level, supposed to be more of a hobby than a business after all. However, when you write out cheques, it is a good discipline to enter all details on the stub and to file paid invoices in a suitable place. Keep

Remember to include any prize money won at shows in with your final accounting.

a note when paying for anything with cash and enter it as soon as possible into your book or computer. Likewise, if you use a credit or debit card to pay your bills, do not forget to include those figures in your record-keeping.

KEEPING BREEDING RECORDS

It is important to keep records relating to breeding and these should show the lineage of your stock, what male was mated with which group of females, and what relationship, if any, they have to each other. To help you with this, it may be necessary to create some sort of 'family tree' or identification system as, although it is possible to make excellent use of double-mating to fix certain desirable features, repeated in-breeding is obviously not conducive to maintaining a strong, healthy strain. It will, in the end, inevitably give rise to as many (if not more) faults as it will good points. An understanding of the potential of breed lines comes about only via experience and a general knowledge of stock.

To help you with this, it may be necessary to create some sort of identification system and this could be by means of toe-punching (not often carried out these days), wing-tagging or, more simply, by the use of leg rings. Adjustable leg rings can be bought from most

Leg rings are a good way of ensuring effective record-keeping.

51

agricultural suppliers and come in various sizes, according to the type of poultry you are keeping. The range of colours allows you to keep colour-coded records – one particular breeding strain might, for example, have yellow leg rings while another pen might have red or purple. Rings are usually made from plastic and are 'spiralled', enabling them to be fitted to birds at any age. Their one disadvantage is that it is possible for the birds to lose them; if you are to have any hope of keeping effective records, it is necessary to keep a few spare rings and replace them just as soon as you notice that one has been lost.

The Poultry Club now operates a closed ring system, which is a far more effective way of doing things. Each of the rings supplied by the club has relevant data stamped on it and represents an excellent way to identify individual birds, not only for your own records, but also as proof of ownership should your stock ever be stolen. Birds have to be ringed when young, so it is not a system that could be applied immediately to existing adult birds.

Wing tags can be coloured or numbered. The tag is positioned at the front of the wing and is covered by feathers so that it is not unsightly and yet can be easily read by parting the feathers.

Should you wish to use toe-punching as a means of identification, this is done in much the same way as livestock is sometimes earmarked. The major disadvantage of the system is that you need to catch individual birds in order to see their particular mark properly.

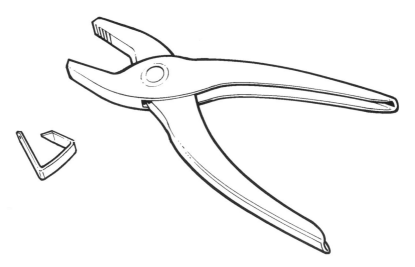

Wing tags are another way of keeping records and can be simply attached by special pliers.

— 4 —

Housing

It is most important that poultry housing in the backyard is reasonably attractive – you do not want to be looking at a 'shanty town' of corrugated tin, and neither do your neighbours. There is no reason why a permanent poultry house should not enhance, rather than detract from, a small plot of land and poultry keepers are well known for their ingenuity when it comes to designing houses!

Devotees of what is known by some as 'the smallholder's bible', *The Complete Book of Self-Sufficiency* by John Seymour (first published in 1976, re-printed several times; most recently in 2003 by Dorling Kindersley), might be tempted to construct one of John's famous

With a little imagination, it is possible to make some unusual and attractive-looking poultry houses that will enhance, rather than detract from, the backyard environment.

home-made arks, from a framework of bent hazel or willow, with a sleeping section covered by overlapping fertilizer sacks. Although adequate, functional and serviceable, such an edifice does not really 'tick all the boxes' when it comes to the subjects of ventilation, condensation, security from predators and aesthetics.

As well as the house itself, the surrounding area can also be made attractive by the inclusion of plant screening, either grown up trellis-work or through the wire netting that goes to make up the run. If this is a possible option, it is essential that the plants or shrubs that are chosen are not of a type or planted in such a way that they will afford easy access to foxes, stoats, rats or cats.

In view of the occasional isolated outbreaks of avian influenza and spasmodic media hype on the subject, you must always consider the need for housing and enclosed runs that are big enough for your poultry to be kept indoors should government requirements ever make this necessary. In most cases, this need be nothing more than a house which is reasonably secure from wild birds and a few pen sections over which a netting roof can be draped.

It is best if outdoor runs can be made so as to prevent access by wild birds, in order to minimize the risk of disease.

ESSENTIAL REQUIREMENTS

Location is all-important and when choosing the site for your poultry unit it is essential to consider several things. Wherever possible, the front of the shed should face south-east. With this orientation, the occupants will get the benefit of the early-morning sun, but by lunchtime the front will be shaded from the hottest weather. Constant winds are to be avoided wherever possible, so pick as sheltered a spot as circumstances will allow, at the same time being aware of the fact that a low-lying place may turn into a mud bath during the wet winter months. All waterfowl must be sheltered from the blazing sun, otherwise they will suffer from heat exhaustion. Hedges and trees cool an area down in a heatwave, and provide shade on the hottest days as well as a little frost protection in the winter.

In a perfect world, the best location would be an orchard or lightly wooded area, but the average backyard poultry fancier is unlikely to have the luxury of such a place. All types of poultry prefer

When considering the ideal location for poultry, full use must be made of any shade-giving trees or a boundary hedge.

woodland; they were, many years ago, forest species and they also exhibit a slight fear of really open spaces due to the fact that their ancestors were more vulnerable to attacks from avian predators in such a situation. If it is possible to include a small tree or bush or two within the 'free-range' area, birds will feel happier and range more freely.

The amount of floor space required in both house and runs will depend to some extent on whether or not your birds will have the opportunity (bird flu restrictions permitting) to do some free-range foraging. As a very general rule, the living space for large heavy birds should be at least 4.5sq m (15sq ft). Small ducks, light chickens and bantams could be given about half this, but, obviously, the more space there is at their disposal, the better poultry will thrive and the less chance there is of disease or other health problems. For extremely large birds such as turkeys, a good general rule of thumb regarding spacing is that one turkey should be given the same amount of space as two chickens. Sufficient space is essential, especially if there is the possibility that you might occasionally need to introduce

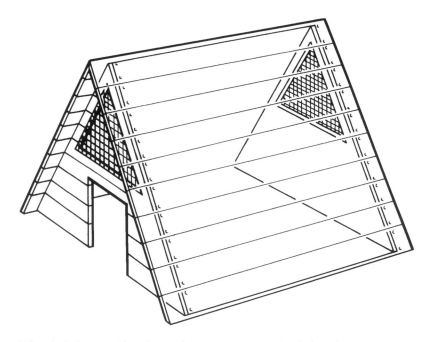

Although the house itself can be quite basic, it is important that ducks and geese are given sufficient ventilation when enclosed for the night.

new birds to an existing flock. Doing this is never easy and they will need time to re-arrange their 'pecking order' before the newcomers are accepted, but they are more likely to adapt if there is enough space for them all. In such a situation, it might be a good idea to create a temporary barrier of sections or wire that will allow birds to become used to one another. After a period of time, the dividing fence can be removed.

Whether the poultry house is quite sophisticated, as in the case of chickens and turkeys, or more basic, as in the case of ducks and geese, one very important consideration is that of adequate ventilation. Without it, hygiene problems are bound to occur and the health of your stock will suffer, resulting in colds, respiratory problems and the very real risk of disease. Having clean fresh air all year round is of great importance but especially during the winter months when even the hardiest of birds will spend a great proportion of their time in the house.

Possibly the simplest way of creating an air flow for the daytime is to have a second, wire-mesh door. This will allow air to enter, but

Wood shavings probably make the best general all-round floor litter and, bought in compressed bales, can be quite cost-effective.

deny access to wild birds and therefore lessen the risk of them con-
taminating your flock with disease. It is not totally fool-proof however, as they may still be able to get through the pop-holes. Also, in
the worst of the winter weather, the solid outer door will need to be
kept shut. Air vents fitted just under the eaves and behind a baffle-
board are good, as are sliding windows fixed over a wire-netting
frame. If the house roof is clad with corrugated sheeting such as
'onduline' – a rubber-based material which screws over the roof and
is both easy to fit and remove (and better than galvanized tin, which
is cold and subject to condensation) – it will create its own ventilation.

A good floor covering is essential. Wood shavings make the best
litter, but leaves collected in the autumn are a good natural alternative, although they are quite bulky to store until needed. Chopped
wheat straw is also a good medium for general poultry keeping.
More modern (and more costly) alternatives are the bales of flax and
shredded newspaper that can be bought from any general agricultural supplier, especially those that deal with the requirements of
horse owners.

CHICKENS AND BANTAMS

Housing Units

Where space allows, a combined house and run that can be moved
periodically on to fresh ground is probably the best option for
chickens and bantams. This type of housing comes in many shapes
and sizes, is easily cleaned, and protects the inhabitants from the
unwanted attentions of foxes and the neighbour's dog. Depending
upon the exact design, the units are known variously as 'fold
units', 'coop and run' or even 'arks' (although, technically, an ark
is a high-pointed 'A'-shaped house traditionally used on free-
range units and, therefore, without a run attachment). The movable house and run system is very versatile and works equally well
when housing mature birds, young stock or a broody hen and her
chicks.

Static houses should be built up off the ground. This has several
advantages: it prevents vermin from taking up residence, allows
extra floor space, gives easy access under the shed for the chickens,
who will welcome it as a dusting area, and keeps the base of the
house dry and less likely to rot.

Any major poultry event is a good place to gain some ideas as to the types of housing that best suit your particular situation.

Planning permission is not normally required prior to constructing a permanent poultry house, but it may pay to contact your local council for specific advice.

Perches

The appropriate height of perches will depend on the type of chickens you want to keep but, as a general rule, they should be about 60cm (2ft) from the ground and not less than 25cm (10in) away from the wall. Ideally, the perches should be made of planed wood so that they are easy to disinfect and less likely to splinter. The tops should be rounded and about 5cm (2in) wide. Allow at least 20cm (8in) of perch space for each bird and, if it is necessary to include more than one perch, ensure that they are all at the same height and at least 36cm (14in) apart.

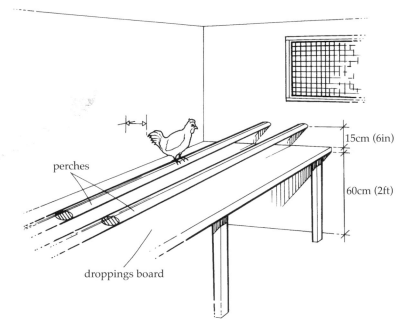

perches

droppings board

15cm (6in)

60cm (2ft)

Perches should not be too high from the ground, must be far enough away from the wall so as not to damage the tail feathers, and may benefit from the addition of a droppings board.

Some poultry keepers like to include a dropping board under the perch area and this certainly makes the daily chore of cleaning out the previous night's droppings much easier. If one is included, it should be set 15cm (6in) below the perches.

Nest Boxes

Nest boxes should be positioned in the darkest part of the house – usually this is directly underneath the windows – and away from the perches so that birds are less inclined to roost in them. Where possible, the nests are best fitted into an outside wall so that they do not take up valuable floor space and can be easily accessed from outside via a hinged (but waterproof) 'roof' or lid.

For large fowl, the box dimensions must be around 60cm (2ft) square. It can be lined with straw, hay, shavings or (perhaps the most hygienic option) shredded paper. There are some keepers who use mixed grit in the box as they believe that a hen will then pick up her necessary grit intake whilst she is laying.

Nest box units may be constructed, perhaps in tiers or as a row of three or four, with each box being enclosed on three sides for privacy. Allow one box for every three birds.

However they are constructed, it is important that nest boxes are kept clean. Faeces in the nest areas should be removed and fresh litter added so that eggs are kept clean. This will prevent the staining of eggs and possible bacterial infection entering via the porous shells. The weather can also have an effect; if the birds are free-range and the weather is wet, dirt can also be transferred to the egg via dirty feet.

Lighting

To lay well, chickens need at least sixteen hours of daylight so, in an effort to maintain a good egg supply during the dark winter months, it will pay to rig up some simple form of lighting. Light stimulates the ovary via the pituitary gland so that more eggs are laid. Also, by extending the feeding time, the chickens have access to more food and will not only lay more eggs, but also larger ones. Artificial light will pay dividends, especially if it is regulated, either in the circuit or at the plug point, by a timer, which can be bought very cheaply from most hardware stores. There is also a product on the market called the Rooster Booster, which monitors a 24-hour pattern of natural light and dark, adjusting itself so that the lights operate only when it becomes dark during any fifteen-hour period. At the end of the day, after a short 'dimming' time, a natural night spell of nine hours commences. Best of all, the system works by being connected to a 12-volt car battery.

Warning

Lighting need not be elaborate and might consist only of a low-wattage bulb run from a car battery. In this case, all is well and good, but if you decide to supply power via an extension from your own home, installation should be carried out only by a professional electrician – rainwater and electricity do not mix! Not only is there the obvious danger aspect to consider but also the fact that, since 2005, although DIY electrical work is still allowed, it must comply with the requirements of 'Part P' of the Building Regulations.

TURKEYS

Accommodation

With limited space available it obviously makes sense to choose smaller breeds of turkey such as Bourbon Reds, and to keep them in a large fold or enclosure, with a roosting house for shelter at night. Housing for turkeys need only be a larger version of that normally provided for chickens. Make sure the pop-hole is large enough to allow the birds an easy entrance and exit.

At one time, the most popular forms of turkey housing were either fold units or 'pole yards', constructed simply of wire netting, poles, corrugated sheeting and three-ply felt. Turkey poults intended for housing in pole barns were usually reared in brooder houses (similar to conventional turkey housing) until six weeks of age, after which time they do not need additional heat. Disadvantages of the system included the fact that they were subject to natural daylight

No matter what type of poultry is being kept, it is important that the pop-holes are large enough to allow birds an easy entrance and exit.

and consequently it was difficult to regulate temperature or ventilation. Injurious pecking was also a problem and had to be controlled by beak-trimming or providing vegetable material and other objects for the turkeys to investigate and amuse themselves.

Perching

In their natural state, turkeys will roost in trees, so they will require some fitted perches. Make sure that the perches are high enough and that they are positioned far enough away from the shed walls so that the birds cannot damage their tails against them. A 5cm (2in)- diameter pole about 60–90cm (2–3ft) high will be adequate. Although turkeys – depending on the type (commercial or standard) – will happily fly up and roost much higher than that, it is important not to encourage such activity as they could damage themselves on the descent if there is not enough room to fly down. The inclusion of a dropping board (*see* page 60) is also a good idea.

Nest Boxes

Turkeys are not as fussy about nest boxes as chickens tend to be, but if boxes are there, they may be used. Ensure that they are wide enough for a bird not to feel too closed in and stressed. A tea chest on its side makes a good nest box, as would an old door or something similar, cut down to about 90cm (3ft) square and leant securely against the shed wall.

DUCKS

One of the big advantages of keeping ducks and geese is that their housing can be very simple: they do not require perches or nest boxes, although they do need adequate ventilation in order to prevent respiratory problems.

Basically, all that is required is a dry house with a raised floor. Ideally, the floor should be constructed of wire mesh or slats, rather than solid boarding, as this will help the chosen litter to drain and prevent the interior from becoming damp and smelly. Because the floor is slatted, it will be impractical to use shavings as litter but, provided the top layer is peeled off at least once a week and replaced by fresh, straw is a good alternative. If you wish to include nest boxes, keep them simple; you may find that the ducks will just lay in the straw litter anyway.

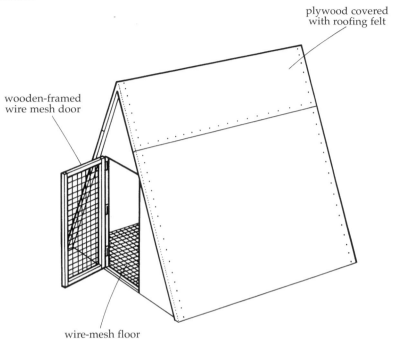

plywood covered
with roofing felt

wooden-framed
wire mesh door

wire-mesh floor

A simply constructed house suitable for ducks and/or geese. (Actual measurements will, of course, vary depending on which is being kept.)

As ducks do not roost, there is no need to provide a house of any great height in order to accommodate perches. A rabbit-hutch-shaped house need be around only 1m (3ft 3in) at the front, dropping to roughly 75cm (2ft 6in) at the back; it is even simpler to construct an 'A'-shaped shed. With either design, a little extra height at the eaves will give better air circulation, especially if the ends of the house are not boarded quite to roof level, and instead are merely protected by the addition of strong wire netting or weld-mesh.

The rabbit-hutch design should have a door at the front, whilst the 'A'-shaped more commonly has a door at one end. Either way, it may pay to fix the door so that it is completely removable, which will help in the weekly clean-out and in keeping the interior smelling more sweetly in warm weather. It has been suggested that a drop-fronted door can double up as an access ramp. (Ducks, being less agile than chickens, will definitely need some form of ramp, especially if the shed is raised any distance from the floor.) In practice, drop-fronted doors are rarely a good idea, as the runners or

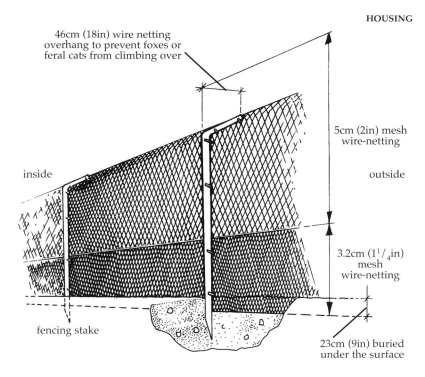

46cm (18in) wire netting overhang to prevent foxes or feral cats from climbing over

5cm (2in) mesh wire-netting

inside

outside

3.2cm ($1^1/_4$in) mesh wire-netting

fencing stake

23cm (9in) buried under the surface

If a duck pen is surrounded by fox-proof fencing, its residents require little or no housing and will be happy enough outdoors.

hinge joints soon become full of debris and refuse to operate efficiently. Probably the best solution is a door that is completely removable, held in place by four 'button' catches.

A house that feels comfortable to the ducks makes shutting them in at night a much easier task. Even so, they will probably need some encouragement most evenings. Any shepherding or herding necessary must be done with the minimum of fuss, as ducks tend to be more excitable than most other types of fowl, responding best to gentle coaxing and kind words.

GEESE

Housing for geese can follow pretty much the same pattern as that for ducks, but obviously the height of the roof or door will require adjusting in order to accommodate the extra height of the birds themselves.

Tom Bartlett, one of the UK's leading experts on keeping ducks and geese, gives some valuable advice in his book *Ducks and Geese: A Guide to Management* (Crowood, 1986):

> Geese need shade in hot weather and, if the area is bleak, benefit greatly from being supplied with some sort of shelter such as wattle hurdles or straw bales. Their housing need only be very simple, with a floor area of about 2m (7ft) square and a height of 1m (3–4ft) for a trio of large geese. Make sure there is plenty of ventilation. Make the ark doors of a mesh big enough to allow plenty of air but small enough to prevent the geese from pushing their heads through. Of course, stables and outbuildings of any kind can make quite satisfactory housing.
>
> One of the most important reasons for housing geese is to protect them from predators, especially foxes. Foxes will be likely visitors, so care must be taken to shut your geese up, well before dusk and not let them out too early in the morning.

Geese reared on grass produce a great deal of droppings and so some form of bedding will be required in the house. Straw is often

Guinea-fowl will be quite happy in semi-confinement, but much prefer being given free-range.

used, but rapidly becomes wet and soggy, generating a great deal of ammonia. Wood shavings are ideal but can prove expensive. Despite the potential problems, you must never leave your birds without bedding, as they will get dirty very quickly. They may even suffer from what is known as 'wet feather', caused by not being able to keep their feathers cleaned, preened and oiled.

GUINEA-FOWL

Although guinea-fowl need no housing and will happily roost in trees, it is sometimes useful to be able to catch them; penning for part of the time will help prevent them from becoming totally wild. With early 'training' (keeping them in their intended home for about a month), it is possible to persuade them to return to a shed each evening in order to roost. Whilst a conventional chicken house is certainly adequate, the backyard poultry keeper who is lucky enough to have a high outbuilding attached to their property will find that birds will prefer to roost on any exposed rafters or beams.

Nest boxes are totally unnecessary for guinea-fowl and will be ignored in favour of a self-chosen, well-hidden nest.

QUAIL

Most quail breeders keep their birds in a caged 'tier' system. The shed in which they are kept must have good ventilation as their droppings are particularly high in ammonia. For continued laying, the lighting regime should be between fourteen and seventeen hours a day and light can also be used to manipulate meat production: if the birds have only eight hours a day their sexual maturity will be delayed and they will eat less but grow faster and fatter while they are not wasting their energies on fighting or mating. Two weeks of extra light will bring quail into breeding condition.

Rabbit hutches can provide ideal housing for quail, but if you want to give them access to an outdoor run it is as well to remember that they are shy, flighty birds. Any netting covering the pen should be of nylon rather than wire so that they do not hurt themselves if they are startled. Each bird should be given an absolute minimum of 200sq cm (30sq in) of floor space. Because of their size, quail are susceptible to attacks from rats, which will kill an entire pen in one night if given the chance. It is therefore essential that the housing and runs are built in such a way as to preclude access by vermin.

OUTDOOR RUNS

All poultry should, wherever possible, be allowed access to the great outdoors. In all but the coldest of conditions, they are much happier and healthier foraging and feeling the sun on their backs than they are quite literally cooped up for the majority of their lives.

The poultry keeper who has only a very small backyard at his disposal has the option of constructing an outdoor run that is wired over the top with 25mm nylon netting as well as up the sides with the normal galvanized variety. However, unless this is sectional so that it can be moved from time to time, there is the very real problem of the ground becoming stale.

Often, too little time is spent in organizing a run so that it can be periodically rested. Probably the easiest way of doing this is either to have a run that is divided and accessed from the house by two separate pop-holes, or to construct two runs, one at either end of the poultry shed. Even though each side is being rested on a regular basis, it is still a good idea annually to cover the area with garden lime so as to keep the soil sweet and assist in preventing the build-

All types of poultry are much happier and healthier when they are given access to grass and sunshine.

up of disease or worms. If liming is carried out in the evening, provided that it rains overnight, the birds can be let out the following day without any fears of risk to their health.

Even new grassland previously devoid of poultry should never be considered clear of potential problems, as wild birds that fly over as well as coming down to feed are continually spreading disease. Free-ranging poultry may be less susceptible to problems, but remember to take into consideration the area immediately surrounding the housing, which will, undoubtedly, become bare and soiled due to the constant passage of the birds and their keeper. Also, land that receives too much nitrogen in the form of poultry droppings becomes acidic and, where this occurs, the grass is unable to recover. The best grass mix is one that contains both grass and clover. Grass for goslings must be clean, short and sweet: provided they are grazed on clean ground containing no poultry parasites, they will grow really well on a diet that consists mainly of grass.

A totally fox-proof pen needs to be high: foxes have, on occasions, been known to clamber over wire any less than 3.65m (12ft) tall. Obviously, to construct such an edifice would be very costly and so most poultry fanciers make do with a fence around 2m (6ft 6in) in height and take extra precautions by fitting insulators approximately 23cm (9in) on to short wooden posts fixed the same distance away from the perimeter fence. Through these is run a single strand of galvanized electric fencing cable attached to an electric energizer. For areas in which poultry are allowed free-range, it will pay to enclose the perimeter with electric netting that will not only prevent predation from foxes hunting in the daytime, but also protect poultry from neighbouring dogs.

PONDS FOR DUCKS AND GEESE

Although a pond is not essential, a 'paddling pool' will enable ducks and geese to keep their eyes and vents clean and also helps with facilitating mating in some breeds. In hot weather, static water can turn green very quickly, so any water source must be easy to drain. If it is supplied by a constant flow of running water, thought must be given as to whether a small duck can squeeze out of either outflow or inflow. Also, will such an arrangement make it easier for predators to gain access?

Making an artificial pond for ducks and geese is not difficult, especially if you use a fibreglass mould from a garden centre.

Although the initial outlay will be more than it would be for a length of butyl liner, it will almost certainly last longer and will look more attractive. To prevent the edge of the pool from becoming muddy, you could use cement or surround the pond with pea shingle, making sure that whatever material is used will not damage the birds' feet. The surround should extend some distance from the edge of the pond and be deep enough not to 'disappear' over time. If the pool is kept full of water, there should be no problem in birds getting out wherever they like, but it is probably a good idea to also include a few steps of breeze-block or bricks submerged just under the water.

The banks of any natural ponds can be planted up with shade-giving shrubbery – this will also help in keeping the banks intact. If possible, it should be planted up before any ducks and geese are introduced to the area; if that is not possible, vegetation should be protected with wire netting; making sure that it is sufficiently tall that a bird cannot scrabble in and become trapped. Sedge-grass and montbretia are good, while some plants, such as *Daphne*, produce poisonous berries and should obviously be avoided.

In a large back garden, it may be possible to create a natural pond for ducks and geese.

— 5 —
Feeding

Correct nutrition of the stock is vital to the backyard poultry keeper. Without it, no bird will breed, grow, lay or put on weight to its best advantage. Birds may, at first glance, look healthy enough, but if there is insufficient protein, minerals, vitamins and calcium in their diet, they will never do really well.

There are all sorts of breeder, rearing and laying rations on the market, for every type of poultry, and these should provide all the essentials required. If you are intending to breed seriously from your birds then you need to consider some of the specialist feeds that are available. These have a better protein and mineral mix for higher fertility and hatchability, and it is possible to purchase specific feeds for breeding chickens and for breeding ducks.

It is important to include grit in the diet of all poultry. A hopper specifically designed for the purpose is a worthwhile investment.

Birds out at grass will find the necessary grit and greenstuffs to support any given diet; if the birds are housed in yards or semi-intensively, however, it is important to include a separate container of mixed grit in order that they can digest their food. Mixed poultry grit is readily available from all agricultural suppliers, but you need to make sure that it contains a good proportion of hard flint grit; pure oyster-shell is too smooth when given on its own and could cause compaction in the digestive system.

There are generally two options when it comes to feeding: hopper and hand-feeding. It is important not to over-feed your birds, as any surplus will encourage fat, unhealthy stock that will neither breed nor lay to their best ability. It also leads to the very real possibility of a plague of vermin such as rats and mice. Given the correct amounts at morning and evening feeds, a programme of hand-feeding is, in the minds of most breeders, the preferential option. Where this is not possible (perhaps due to commitments of work), a compromise of pellets or mash fed in a hopper and an evening scattering of grain may have to be made.

When hand-feeding, it is important that you ensure that the amount of food is exactly right. It is elementary really: if you find no trace of food left an hour or so after breakfast, increase the amount

For practical reasons, hopper-feeding may be your only option, but, in the interests of bio-security, the hoppers are best placed inside the house rather than in the open air, as seen here.

until the last particles are being picked up around lunchtime. If there is food left from the morning when you take the afternoon feed out, then obviously it will be necessary to decrease accordingly the amount given at breakfast. The amount of food that is required depends on the type and varieties of breeds, their stage of development, the methods and environment chosen to house your birds and the time of year.

Never let your birds go without clean fresh water: the quantity that they will drink in a day depends on the time of year, the type of food being given and the size of the bird. Again, you must be the best judge of how much your flock drinks and this can only be estimated by careful observation on your part. In the case of ducks and geese, avoid creating potential problems by preventing access to stagnant marshy areas, where rotting vegetation can cause botulism and possibly death.

CHICKENS AND BANTAMS

Poultry have different nutritional requirements according to their age. Young chickens that have not yet reached point-of-lay need much more protein. This is best provided by the use of chick

Young chicks will only do well if given the correct food, containing all the necessary nutritional requirements.

crumbs, starter pellets and grower's pellets before finally weaning them on to an adult ration.

It is not easy to say exactly how much complete feed chickens and bantams should receive as this depends not only upon the size of the bird, but also on one or two external factors. In winter, for example, a chicken needs more food than it does in the summer in order to retain the correct body temperature. Likewise, a broody hen will hardly eat anything during the time she is sitting; the food that she does eat should be predominantly grain-based. As a general rule, however, you should accept that a fully grown large fowl will consume around 30–100g (1–3$^1/_2$ oz) per day, of which just less than half should be a mixture of wheat and maize (*see* 'Feed Options', below).

Laying hens may well prefer the corn feed, but if this becomes the main part of the diet then the protein levels that the bird is getting decline and her ability to be a good producer is compromised. This is especially important in young birds coming into lay. This is a time of maturation and a lack of all the best nutrition can slow down the onset of lay, and produce birds that are poorer in general. Most free-ranging birds do not need an 18 per cent feed like those in the more intensive units: insects; grubs and seeds will supplement the usual free-range layer's meal or pellets, which are 16 per cent protein.

A variety of old-fashioned and less-than-efficient chick and poultry feeders — even if they are still obtainable, they are not to be recommended.

Young chicks are best fed on proprietary chick crumbs developed specifically for the purpose. They are very susceptible to disease when young and most feeds have a good antibiotic in the right concentration to protect them against coccidiosis, which can be a major chick killer. Make sure that the crumbs are always available and easily accessible. When rearing under a brooder, it may pay to use Keyes trays as feeders for the first week or so, until they are big enough to get at a long chick feeder. It is also important to provide proper chick grit for very young birds in order to prevent the possibility of gizzard impaction.

DUCKS

Feeding ducks is as simple as sorting out their housing: they will thrive on a basic diet of crumbly wet mash and a separate feed of grain in the evening. Beware of providing more mash than the birds can eat in one session, as moist mash has the unfortunate habit of quickly becoming stale and sour, especially in warm weather. There is no reason why poultry pellets should not be used but the ideal is a well-balanced waterfowl or game-bird ration. Make sure that it is

Ducklings should be kept away from anything other than drinking water until they are at least partially feathered.

free from additives: for some reason, anti-coccidiostats, for example, are detrimental to the well-being of ducks.

Be very wary of feeding ducklings medicated chick crumbs unless you really cannot get anything else. They eat a lot more than chicks and so can end up getting too high a dose of the antibiotic, which can be lethal. If you only have a few ducklings to rear they appear to thrive on a cereal-based dog food, which should at first be mashed into a shallow saucer with a little water combined.

Confined birds will benefit from being given a few extra treats, as they are unable to free-range and thus supplement their diet. Earthworms, mealworms, slugs and peanuts are all eagerly devoured, but beware of a fungus that can sometimes be found in badly stored peanuts, which can affect the health of ducks in particular and poultry in general. Cooked vegetables and brown bread are also appreciated and do not forget a regular supply of mixed grit, as penned birds are obviously unable to source their own.

Drinking water is best given in troughs or fountains, and the ducks should not have access to the source, otherwise they will just treat it as a pond. Water needs to be supplied in both the house and run, because, unlike other types of poultry, ducks will eat and drink at night. It also needs to be regularly changed, or it will quickly become fouled. Ducks of all breeds like to eat and drink alternately, often actually dunking their food in the water before eating.

GEESE

It should not be necessary to feed adult geese at all during the spring, summer and early autumn months, provided that they have access to as much short, sweet grass as possible. Large strains of growing geese will require at least 0.5kg (1lb) of mixed grain and pellet per day if their grazing is restricted and that is not good for their welfare; if supplementary feeding can be kept to a minimum it will benefit both the birds and your pocket. It is essential, however, to provide plenty of sand and grit so that the gizzard can function properly. If you are fattening birds for the table, geese are traditionally kept confined with just grain to eat for a fortnight before slaughter.

Goslings can be fed in much the same way as ducklings and, even if they are being reared by their natural mother, they will require some supplementary feeding such as chick crumbs or mash. This can get quite expensive, as it will not be long before mum, dad and any 'aunts' are also pitching in!

In situations where geese and ducks do not have access to a pool or stream, it is advisable to move drinkers on to a new location each day. When drinkers stay in the same location for too long, the land around them can rapidly become overgrazed, muddy, and filthy with droppings, particularly during the winter season.

TURKEYS

Turkeys are easy to feed, and it is probably not necessary to go to the trouble that some turkey fanciers took in the past. When fattening their stock for the table, some felt that it was advantageous to make sure that 'their first food after hatching should consist of fresh sweet meal, soft custard made with equal parts of egg and milk set by a gentle heat, and, above all, an abundance of some bitter milky herb, such as dandelion or, much better, lettuce running to seed' (William Cobbett, writing in 1823).

Young turkeys require a higher level of protein (27–28 per cent) than most other types of fowl and so it is important to feed them on turkey or game starter crumbs at day-old before progressing to grower's pellets at around six weeks of age. Some feed manufacturers have a turkey rearer pellet available, which is similar in content

A mature Norfolk stag — the traditional Christmas turkey!

to the grower's pellet, but smaller in size. A little wheat can be given at around twelve weeks; however, if the turkeys are intended as table birds, they will also need to be fed a finisher ration from around sixteen weeks.

Plenty of fresh, clean water is essential and, if the birds can be given access to an outside run, they will thrive on grass and the exercise will certainly help their development.

GUINEA-FOWL

Guinea-fowl are very easy to keep and there is little to say about any specific feeding or dietary habits. Young birds will do extremely well on the regime outlined for turkeys, but, generally, they can be fed a diet similar to that suggested for chickens and bantams. Ranging guinea-fowl will find a great deal of their food naturally and they are more interested in insects and bugs than they are in anything vegetable; clearly, this makes them ideal for the backyard poultry keeper who may be worried about his prize vegetable plot.

QUAIL

It is possible, but by no means easy, to source proprietary quail food. If a standard ration for either growing or breeding quail is not available commercially, good-quality, fresh, commercial turkey or game-bird diets are recommended, preferably fed as crumb in order to minimize feed wastage.

Breeding quail are best fed a game-bird breeder's ration based on a 19–20 per cent protein level, at the rate of 25g ($^3/_4$oz) per day. For the first six weeks quail should be fed a diet containing approximately 25 per cent protein. A good-quality commercial starter ration for game birds or turkeys contains 25–28 per cent protein. If this is not available, a chicken starter ration (20–22 per cent protein) can be used, but the birds will grow more slowly. Growing birds do much better on small crumbs than they do on meal. Laying diets should contain about 24 per cent protein.

Small stocks of quail will do very well on a staple diet of mixed canary seed, millet and chick crumbs, with a green supplement that might include shredded lettuce and alfalfa. All should be given shell grit or ground limestone after the age of about five weeks.

Adult Japanese quail eat 14–18g ($^1/_2$–$^2/_3$oz) of food per day and require roughly 1.25–2.5cm ($^1/_2$–1in) of feeder space per bird. Clean,

An automatic watering system suitable for small breeds such as quail.

fresh water should be provided at all times and nipple drinkers and cups are especially suitable for adult quail. One nipple or cup should be provided for every five birds, but a small jam-jar type water dish with some pebbles placed in the bottom opening is a useful way of preventing young quail chicks from drowning in the early stages.

FEED OPTIONS

The mixing and feeding of all the required basics of a chicken's diet is a fine art and it is unnecessary to produce a perfect home-made mix now that balanced foods are readily available; in any case, it is impossible. For those worried about the unknown additives connected with the manufacture of commercial poultry foods, it is as well to realize that free-range and organic rations are available, which do not contain such undesirable components. Whatever your choice, it is essential that you buy foodstuffs of excellent quality from firms of reputation.

If, for any reason, you wish to change the type of food given, the process must be done slowly over a period of seven to ten days. Any changeover should follow roughly the same pattern: mix in around a quarter volume of the new food to three-quarters of the old for

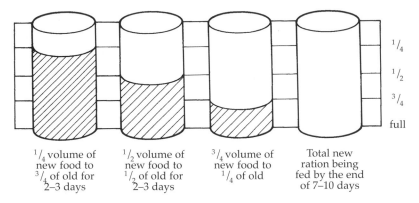

$^1/_4$

$^1/_2$

$^3/_4$

full

| $^1/_4$ volume of new food to $^3/_4$ of old for 2–3 days | $^1/_2$ volume of new food to $^1/_2$ of old for 2–3 days | $^3/_4$ volume of new food to $^1/_4$ of old | Total new ration being fed by the end of 7–10 days |

Any change in diet should be introduced gradually over a period of time.

two or three days; then, mix half and half for the same amount of time; next, give three-quarters of the new food mixed with a quarter of the old before finally changing entirely to the new ration.

Pellets and Mash

Pellets are easier to manage and possibly less wasteful, but some experienced poultry keepers feel that it is better to feed a dry mash than a pellet. Their argument is that, as it takes chickens around three hours of continuous feeding to eat the amount of mash they require, it will keep them entertained much better than a day's ration of pellets, which can be consumed in half an hour. When they are fed pellets, chickens may well become bored, especially during the winter months.

Where mash is being used, it is important to stir it well before feeding: studies have found that ingredients such as ground limestone, which is included as a source of calcium, tend to sift through the food and settle at the bottom of the bag. Birds given food from the top of the bag may, therefore, miss out on some of these vital components. There can be no doubt that mash is a messier form of feeding.

Cereal Feeds

Being harder to digest, cereal is best given as the afternoon or early-evening feed, thus ensuring that birds go to roost with a full crop. The best mix is one of wheat and maize but the ratio should not be more than roughly one-quarter maize to three-quarters wheat. A little more maize can, however, be fed during the winter months, as it is an excellent way of maintaining the bird's body heat.

Too much maize in a laying bird's diet is bad for its health and fatty deposits can build up around the ovaries. On the other hand, a high maize diet will fatten table birds more quickly and give their flesh the 'corn-fed' colour that is seen on the best of organic supermarket chickens, and commands a premium. Split maize is a very useful tool in enhancing the colour of yellow-legged breeds that are intended for showing and its inclusion in their diet will often sharpen up 'faded' legs. It also improves the colour of egg yolks.

Household Scraps

For maximum egg production, household scraps should form not more than 20 per cent of the daily total intake, but some readers, keen on recycling and self-sufficiency, may wish to use their leftovers. One way of doing this would be to boil up any vegetable scraps and add them to mash. If you decide on this method of feeding, it is important that you make the resultant mixture moist but crumbly, and not sloppy. If the mash breaks up easily when a mixing spoon is put through it, you have got it about right.

Household scraps can be a useful addition to the diet of any surplus stock being brought on as table birds.

If you are raising some surplus cockerels for the table, household scraps can be an invaluable addition to their diet and will certainly help in bulking up flesh when fed along with a high-protein proprietary fattening meal. The meat on a bird fed in this way will have a great deal more taste than that on the majority of commercially produced chickens; a varied diet (this is where you can use maize to great advantage) will make the carcass virtually self-basting.

Your birds will also enjoy any leftover stale brown bread soaked in milk (white is as unhealthy for poultry as it is for humans), as well as cheese, rice, pasta and any cereal-based scraps. However, you should not feed strong-tasting, mouldy or otherwise contaminated food, as this will at the very least taint the eggs and at the worst cause digestive problems and even death.

Greenstuffs

Free-ranging birds will get most of their greenstuffs naturally. In the early part of the season, grass that has been correctly managed will be high in chlorophyll, which has, like split maize, been found to be beneficial in improving the colour tone of yellow-legged chickens.

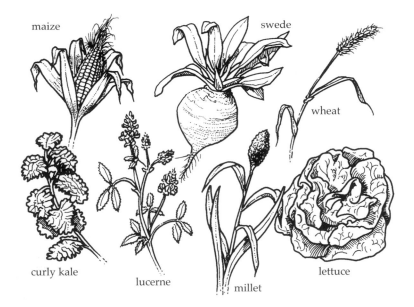

A selection of plants worth growing in the vegetable patch for feeding as greenstuffs to poultry.

Many of the outer leaves of cabbage, cauliflower, beet, lettuce and sprouts that are intended for use in the kitchen can also all be given to chickens and will form a very important part of their daily diet of greenstuffs.

In grassless runs and houses, a few turfs of short grass can be thrown in at intervals, but it is far better to give your birds a regular daily supply of greenstuffs, which, for preference, should be hung off the ground or given in racks. Whatever method is chosen, any leftovers must be removed each night and placed on the compost heap. If you have space in your garden, many crops can be grown especially for feeding to poultry. Useful varieties include lucerne, vetches, green cereals, rape, kale, millet, sorrel, chard and clover. Always try and give them the whole plant, as chickens will find grubs and minerals in the soil surrounding the roots as well as in the leaves and stems.

As long as they have no chance of being contaminated by chemicals or car exhausts, weeds gathered in the countryside can also be a good addition to the diet. Poultry are good at balancing their own nutritional needs: milkweed, thistle seeds, elder, hawthorn and blackberries seem to be particular favourites. Fortunately, they also seem to have enough common sense not to attempt to eat poisonous garden plants such as laburnum, yew, monkshood and ivy.

VITAMINS

Vitamin and mineral supplements are available commercially but are not normally required because the manufacturers of pellets and mash always add a certain amount. There may, however, be certain times of the year – during the winter months, rearing periods and at the moult, for example – when additional vitamins may prove beneficial.

During breeding periods and also in the moult most types of poultry will benefit from some extra TLC. Giving extra vitamins can do no harm and, although it is possible to find a huge and confusing array of products on the market, perhaps the simplest solution is to administer a good-quality multi-vitamin in either the food or water supply. For preference, choose those that are water-soluble: poultry will always drink and this ensures a fair distribution throughout the flock. Vitamins given in food will tend to settle in the bottom of the feed trough, but you can overcome this problem by mixing a tiny amount of cod-liver oil into the daily ration. This enables the powder to stick to the food and the result is that the supplement is more likely to be evenly distributed amongst the birds.

> ## Warning
>
> It is essential that sufficient vitamins are included in the diet of your breeding stock, otherwise the resulting chicks may hatch with curly, misshapen toes, splayed legs, twisted necks and breastbones. It is, however, important to note that similar defects in incubator-hatched birds may be a result of bad incubator management and have nothing to do with genetic deficiencies.

There are some excellent vitamins on the market – 'Solvit' is one example – and, as they have a long shelf life, it is useful to have a sachet or two always on hand. Be sure to follow the vet's or manufacturer's instructions to the letter and always discard any medicated water that is over 24 hours old.

FEEDERS AND DRINKERS

There are dozens of types of feeders and drinkers, ranging from cheap plastic affairs to grandiose works of art that look like sculptures. Some are just a basic trough whilst others can be controlled remotely and set to distribute food at given times throughout the day. The type you eventually choose depends entirely on its suitability for the particular job in hand and how deeply you might have to delve in your pocket.

More important is the way in which they are used. Make sure that the area around feeders and drinkers is kept clean – any soiled litter should be removed and replaced as part of the daily routine. It should also go without saying that all feeders and drinkers must be cleaned regularly. Before the very real threat of avian influenza, it was common to feed birds outside, but it is nowadays best to follow DEFRA's advice of feeding indoors, to reduce the risk of contamination of feed by wild birds.

Place feeders and drinkers off the ground, preferably on raised slatted platforms, as this will help to avoid damp areas. Raking the floor litter on a regular basis is also recommended as it introduces air and avoids matting.

The number of feeders is also important – just because a feeder has feed in it does not mean that all birds are feeding adequately. Having several smaller hoppers rather than one large one will ensure that all are getting an equal chance to fill their crops without being bullied.

Although chickens like to scratch for corn, waterfowl are definitely better fed in deep containers, to limit spillage and wastage. They are not inclined to search for food like the hens, preferring to scoop up mouthfuls rather than search for grains. Spilled pellets are therefore wasted or become mouldy, creating another potential health hazard.

STORING FEED

It is important to obtain fresh feed, and to store it in covered containers with tightly fitting lids in a clean, dry, cool area that is free from animals and vermin.

Always buy your feed from a busy store that is known to have a good turnover of poultry products. At this sort of place, there is less chance of buying stock that has gone stale or even beyond its 'sell-by' date. Feed stored for longer than eight weeks is subject to vitamin deterioration and rancidity, especially during the summer months. Any cereal or seed (peanuts, linseed and the like) bought as

Two excellent examples of large hopper feeders.

a 'treat' for the birds must be clean and shiny in appearance and should not smell musty or contain any dust.

The temperature and humidity of the place where you store your food is also important, as is the need to keep the area clean, well lit and ventilated with fresh air. Store bags on a pallet so that air can circulate and keep the edges of the bags well away from the walls, especially if they are tin, brick or concrete, where moisture and condensation are likely to be a problem. The backyard poultry keeper whose land allows him to keep a fair number of birds, who therefore needs to buy in bulk, should also take care not to store more than ten bags on each pallet.

It is also a good idea to design the storage area to facilitate a FIFO ('first in first out') system, with bags stored in consecutive order so that the oldest can be withdrawn first. It is too easy to empty the place nearest to the door, replenish that space with 'fresh' food and then use that first again, leaving older bags to go stale at the back of the building.

Check that the contents of each bag are clearly marked and that all possess the paper label stitched into the bag when packed. This label contains vital information, such as the date manufactured, the percentage level of individual ingredients, drugs included and, perhaps most important of all, their expiry date.

Food should be stored in airtight and vermin-proof containers in order to prevent it becoming stale and soiled.

— 6 —
Breeding, Hatching
and Rearing

Generally, breeding pens should be quiet and sheltered from cold winds: in some situations, it may pay to surround the bottom of the runs with weatherboard protection, corrugated sheets or, possibly the simplest and most effective, the small-meshed nylon wind-break material that can be obtained by the roll from all garden centres.

Wherever pens of breeding stock are kept alongside each other, some form of screen is essential in order to prevent the males from spending more time 'sparring' up to each other than mating with the females.

Without some sort of partition dividing breeding pens, birds are more likely to become stressed and spend time fighting through the wire.

You need to take great care when creating breeding pens of birds. No matter how vigorous the ancestors of domestic strains of poultry might have been in the wild, most have been bred closely so as to create a desired type. As a result, there has already been a great deal of in-breeding and it is important that you are not responsible for continuing the trend, thereby undoubtedly causing greater problems for future generations. If, for example, brother and sister are used from parents who were also brother and sister, it is inevitable that genetic faults will be seen in the ensuing offspring. Breeding pairs need to be genetically compatible and this is especially important in geese. Always keep a record (*see* Chapter 3) in order to ensure that you know exactly what has been mated with what.

Individual birds must be carefully chosen for inclusion in a breeding pen. If good-quality pure breeds are the desired aim, it is essential to know the standards. Waterfowl standards are published regularly by the British Waterfowl Association and the Poultry Club standards cover all major breeds of poultry, including turkeys. Check male chickens for the length of their spurs; if they are too long, they should be carefully trimmed in order not to damage the females when mating, or 'treading'. When breeding turkeys, the hens should be fitted with purpose-made leather or canvas saddles prior to the breeding season in order to protect them from the males'

Shown here protecting the backs of Blue Orpington females, saddles are used on either chickens or turkeys to prevent damage when mating.

spurs. The saddle should be fitted 'ridge side' up – many novice breeders make the elementary mistake of doing the opposite, which does not provide the same level of protection.

CHICKENS AND BANTAMS

Most breeds of chickens and bantams are polygamous but some, such as the Sumatras and a number of the game breeds, are virtually monogamous and it is important to realize the difference when it comes to creating a breeding ratio that ensures the optimum hatchability of every egg laid. Because of their weight and shape, the Cornish or Jubilee Game, for example, find it difficult to mate successfully and so no more than a pair or trio should be kept together. Generally, the ratio of females per male depends on the breed – with heavy easy-going breeds such as Rhode Island Reds or Wyandottes, it is normal to run two to five hens with one cockerel, whereas, with a highly active Mediterranean breed such as the Leghorn, it is possible to increase the number to as many as eight or ten females to one cock bird.

Even when the breeding pen is, to all intents and purposes, perfect to the human eye, quite often one or two hens will lay infertile

A Silver-Pencilled Wyandotte cock bantam with his harem – the number of hens a male bird can cope with depends to some extent on the breed.

eggs due to the simple fact that the cock bird does not 'fancy' them. The age of the birds will also affect fertility and it is important not to breed from stock that is either too young (less than a year) or too old (more than five or six years).

DUCKS

Water is not essential when keeping ducks and geese, other than that for drinking and cleanliness, but mating in the wild is almost always carried out on water and the fertility of domestic ducks will be improved if they have access to it.

A breeding pen should consist of one drake to six or seven ducks and you should be aware of the fact that some drakes become very aggressive towards their females during the breeding season. This problem is more likely to occur when there is competition between males, either in the same pen or when they are housed next door to each other.

Two-year-olds in both ducks and geese are better breeders than younger birds, which might be immature. This is especially important in table breeds where it might reasonably be assumed that size is wanted. Size is easily lost by using small eggs from first-year birds. Older ducks are less productive and shell quality tends to decline in birds of more than four years of age. Drakes, on the other hand, have a longer breeding life, especially those of the light breeds.

Unlike geese, ducks make very poor mothers and it is advisable to collect and hatch their fertile eggs under a broody hen or in an incubator.

GEESE

Like ducks, geese will breed more successfully if they have water on which to copulate. If it is not available, this should not prevent breeding, except in the case of the really heavy breeds, such as the Embden and Toulouse, where the provision of water will assist in mating.

One gander to four geese is the accepted ratio and it is important that they are all introduced at the same time. Trying to bring in a bird at a later date will often result in the newcomer being ostracized and ignored. Unlike ducks, where the drake will mate with a female at first sight, a gander will not always mate until he has become settled with his 'harem', so it is essential that they are kept together for at least five to six weeks prior to the time when any fertile eggs are required.

Also unlike ducks, the goose makes an excellent mother and it is possible to leave her to brood her own eggs and look after the goslings once they are hatched.

Given the opportunity, geese normally make their own nests outside but, when confined, are not averse to sitting happily in a quiet corner of the shed or night shelter. It is not unknown for geese to share the same nest and in such a situation, where this is possible, it is advisable to mark the eggs on which the goose is sitting with a heavy pencil mark. In this way, any freshly laid eggs (which will obviously be unmarked) can be collected and removed, leaving behind only the ones to be hatched.

TURKEYS

When breeding from traditional breeds rather than the huge commercial varieties, there should be no problem with the male bird mating with the female and subsequently producing fertile eggs. A turkey stag or 'Tom' can be a little aggressive in his mating habits, hence the need to equip the female with a leather or canvas saddle (*see* pages 88–89). Turkey enthusiasts will often breed from a single pair, but a trio or quartet of birds can also prove successful.

After laying on a regular basis for several weeks, natural survival instincts ensure that a female goes broody. Turkey hens make good sitters; they were, for a long time, used quite commonly in France to hatch successions of hen eggs. At first, it may not be clear that a hen is going broody, but tell-tale signs include persistent nesting, hissing, and walking on 'tip-toes'. She will, like all types of poultry, be anxious to try and return to the nest despite being forcibly removed or otherwise disturbed. Again, like most types of poultry (with the possible exception of geese, who will sit quite happily on a clutch of eggs in situ), once thoroughly broody, a hen turkey can be moved to a quiet comfortable place where she can sit on a clutch of eggs without being unduly disturbed.

GUINEA-FOWL

A breeding pen of guinea-fowl should consist of one cock bird to four or five hens. Once such a group has formed, it will remain the

Most female turkeys will sit on their own eggs and make good mothers.

same and, if the birds are mixed into a larger flock to over-winter, it will re-group in the same combination the following spring. Rearing from day-old is the only sure way to start a flock of guinea-fowl because breeding birds bought as adults are very difficult to integrate. Taken to its logical conclusion, however, this fact could eventually cause problems several generations down the line, by which time the flock will be severely inter-bred. The fertility of eggs laid by free-range guinea-fowl hens has been proven to be higher than in situations where a breeding flock is kept totally penned or enclosed.

Unless the female can sit on a nest of her own making, usually in a hedgerow or similar out-of-the-way place, she will, nine times out of ten, desert an artificial nest; in this case, it is probably best to hatch her eggs under a broody or in an incubator. It has been suggested that a broody turkey hen will make a better foster mother for guinea-fowl 'keets', due to the fact that she will keep them banded together until the following spring, whereas a broody chicken or bantam will tend to ignore them after about six weeks.

QUAIL

Traditionally, breeding quail are kept in trios or quartets, but better fertility seems to be achieved when each pen contains three cock birds, each of which should be provided with one or two females. Flock mating is possible, but, in such a situation, it is advisable to have fewer males in order to reduce the possibility of fighting: a ratio of one male to four or five females is ideal. Their fertility is reduced after about 16 weeks and is even lower when they have been laying for six months or more. It is important to bear this fact in mind if you are considering a serious breeding programme.

Breeding stock need a warm environment of 15.5–21°C (60–70°F) and the house or shed must be well ventilated, as their droppings are particularly high in ammonia. Wire-floored cages make the best breeding units for one cock and three or four hens; the dimensions should be around (and certainly no less than) 60cm (2ft) square and 30cm (1ft) high.

Male quail are quite easy to sex: apart from the attractive deep orange/red throat, he can be identified at breeding time by a secretion of a white 'foam ball', which is a urinary product looking not unlike shaving foam and indicates fertility.

A small incubator, which will successfully hatch quail eggs and takes up very little space, may be a precious commodity to the backyard poultry keeper.

Even when kept in ideal conditions, Japanese quail very rarely go broody and it is almost always necessary to hatch and rear them under small broody bantams such as a Silkie or Silkie cross. It is, however, more normal for them to be hatched in incubators and reared under brooders.

HATCHING

If space permits and it is possible to hatch eggs under a broody hen or bantam, then you are strongly advised to do so. The hen is naturally more experienced at the job than even the most knowledgeable of incubator users and there are no problems concerning temperatures, humidity, egg-turning and all the other potential difficulties that may beset those attempting to hatch artificially for the first time. Incubators undoubtedly have their place in the backyard, and the novice poultry breeder who wants to make use of one will find invaluable *The New Incubation Book* by Dr A.F. Anderson Brown and G.E.S. Robbins (Hancock House Publishers, 2002).

A broody bantam is undoubtedly the best option when only a few chicks are required each year.

With Broody Hens

It is important to choose the broody hen with great care. Although some of the lighter breeds will go broody, they are less inclined to remain so for the required period of time, and it is far better to use one of the heavier breeds or even a cross-breed (who, it must be said, quite often make the best broodies and foster mothers). Having said that, however, it is not necessarily a good idea to use a bird that is too heavy to cover small eggs; she will probably be too clumsy and a bantam will undoubtedly be the better option.

The best place to keep a broody hen whilst sitting is in a coop and run that is situated in a quiet corner, well away from distractions and disturbance. Alternatively, it might be possible to sit her on her own nest in the corner of a larger shed or outbuilding until the chicks are hatched. Whatever method is chosen, the box should be the same dimensions as an ordinary nest box and approximately 60cm (2ft) square. An upturned grass sod or some fine damp earth should be included at the base of the box as this will help form a 'saucer' for the nest and also provide much-needed humidity. On top of the soil, build up a nest of hay or straw (hay for preference),

'Dummy' eggs are useful when encouraging young birds to lay in designated nest boxes and also whilst settling a broody hen on to a new nest.

and be sure to pack it tightly into the corners so that no eggs can roll out. Dust the nest with flea powder. Make sure that the broody is ready to sit by first introducing her to a nest of 'dummy' eggs for twenty-four hours.

Do not over-face the hen by giving her too many eggs to cover. There is a very real danger that the eggs will become chilled due to the fact that, as the hen attempts to turn them, they will be pushed away from the 'brood spot' – the place directly under the breast of the bird, which provides the perfect temperature. It should be possible to accommodate four or five goose eggs under a large hen; the actual number will, of course, depend on the size of eggs and the size of hen.

The hen should be allowed or lifted off the eggs once a day for food, water and the opportunity to evacuate her bowels (any faeces in the nest must be immediately removed, to prevent the eggs becoming soiled). A hen will use her beak and feet to regularly turn any 'normal'-sized eggs placed under her but, if she is required to sit on either turkey or goose eggs, they should be turned by hand when the broody is off the nest. For the first week, ten minutes a day is all that she should be allowed but, after that, the time can be increased up about twenty minutes. On the eighteenth (twentieth if

A traditional broody coop suitable for most situations.

hatching geese or turkeys) and each succeeding day, it will pay to damp down both nest and eggs with aired water.

Incubators

If you wish to control the timing of your hatch or are unable to source a ready supply of broody hens when they are needed, there is no alternative but to use an incubator. These come in various shapes and sizes, and each will have specific hatching instructions as recommended by the manufacturer. Some of the smaller or older types might require the eggs to be turned twice daily by hand, but others are equipped with an egg-turning or tilt mechanism on a timer.

Make sure that the incubator is housed in a suitable shed or outbuilding, where a constant temperature may be retained. Modern electric units are nowadays so compact that it is tempting to situate them in a spare bedroom or study; but central heating and a stale air flow will affect the results. A brick building with good insulation is

After a few hours, newly hatched chicks lose the 'egg tooth' at the tip of the beak.

likely to produce a better hatch than a draughty wooden shed or, worse still, a tin one, where the temperature will fluctuate dramatically every time the sun shines. The ideal temperature is 16–21°C (60–70°F). Adequate ventilation is also important and if a room feels at all stuffy it could be affecting the eggs. A concrete floor is a good idea – not only is it easier to clean and disinfect, but also, as hatching time approaches, it can, if necessary, be kept damp so as to improve humidity in the incubator.

Duck eggs set in incubators need special attention. In dry regions, spraying daily with tepid water from the tenth day of incubation will prove beneficial to the hatching percentage. In places where atmospheric humidity is normally high – in areas of above-average rainfall – any additional moisture is probably not necessary.

When using an incubator, it is never a good idea to mix eggs from different varieties of poultry, not just because of the obvious difference in hatching times, but also because a mixture of eggs will affect the temperature and humidity of the incubator at hatching time, as well as increasing the risk of disease.

REARING

Always start with clean quarters: any small building, garage or corner can be used as a brooding area, as long as it is warm, draughtproof and rodent-free – there is nothing rats like better than young poultry chicks, especially ducklings and goslings. Where possible, it is obviously easier and the results will be better if chicks are reared under a broody hen. A broody hen will accept chicks that have not

---

Hatching Times

Bantams	19–21* days
Chickens	21
Ducks	28
Geese	28–35*
Turkeys	28
Guinea-fowl	28
Quail	18–22*

*Depending on breed.

---

been hatched by her as long as they are introduced carefully. Let her sit on a nest of dummy or infertile eggs for a week and then, on the evening when the chicks arrive, take one and place it under her breast feathers. If she takes to this one, wait an hour or so before introducing the others.

Artificial hatching, however, generally necessitates artificial brooding. At first, the method most commonly used was what might be termed the 'coverlet' system, whereby material such as strips of flannel or wool, warmed from above, was provided for chicks to nestle under, as they would under the feathers of a hen. This method was used for several years, but chick losses were quite considerable due to confinement, variable heat levels and pollution caused by the chicks continually breathing stale air. The system has now been abandoned and there are many varieties of artificial brooder on the market. In some, heated wiring traverses the upper part of the chamber, some inches above the chicks; in others, a warm iron plate radiates heat in the same way or warmed air is brought in by a system of flues and openings. In some very small brooders, the heat is supplied by a simple lamp suspended above the chicks, but

A 'vintage' poultry brooder, nowadays looked upon as a museum piece.

in all there should be a warmed shelter of some type, which might lead into a sheltered but unheated outer chamber. This aids the eventual transition to exposure to the outside weather.

For small numbers of birds all you need is a large cardboard box, some shavings, a heat lamp, a feeder and water. The brooding area should be dry, reasonably well lit and ventilated, and free from draughts. Cover the floor with a few inches of absorbent litter material, such as wood shavings, under which you should place a layer of paper sacks or newspaper. Good management will require the removal of wet spots and addition of clean, dry litter on a regular basis.

Chickens and Bantams

If chicks have been hatched under a broody hen, there is very little left for the backyard poultry keeper to do other than transfer them on to fresh ground, give them clean litter and provide a ready supply of proprietary chick crumbs, together with a safe vessel of water in which the young birds cannot drown. The hen will do the rest.

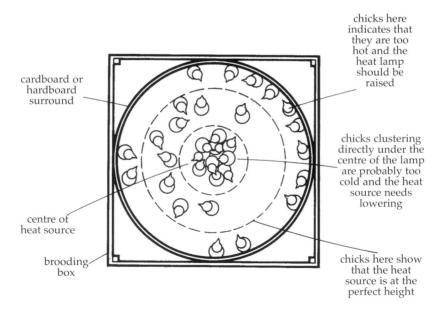

chicks here indicates that they are too hot and the heat lamp should be raised

cardboard or hardboard surround

chicks clustering directly under the centre of the lamp are probably too cold and the heat source needs lowering

centre of heat source

brooding box

chicks here show that the heat source is at the perfect height

By watching the position of chicks under a brooding lamp, it should be possible to tell whether they are too hot or too cold, and to adjust the height of the lamp accordingly.

Once your chicks have hatched in the incubator, leave them for a couple of hours to dry off and then transfer them to a brooding pen or hutch. The simplest arrangement is a small rectangle with wooden walls laid over newspaper on the floor of a garage or shed. The 'walls' need only be 30–60cm (1–2ft) high and a wire-mesh top will prevent the occupants from jumping out. For most chicks, an ordinary 60- or 100-watt light bulb will be perfectly adequate. Begin with the bulb positioned about 18cm (7in) from the floor and adjust the height by observing the behaviour of the birds. If they huddle together beneath the bulb, it needs to be lowered; if they stay at the perimeter of their pen, the bulb should be raised. Keep the bulb on constantly for the first two weeks, raising it slightly every three days or so. During week three, turn it off for an hour on day one, two hours on day two, and so on, and then, at the start of the fourth week, provide heat only during the hours of darkness.

Ducks

As with all types of poultry, it is obviously far easier to hatch and rear ducklings under a broody, but if there is no alternative, incubator hatching and artificial brooding works well.

When rearing under artificial brooders, remember that ducklings do not need as high a temperature as other forms of domestic fowl; a heat pattern of around 30°C (86°F) is ideal for the first few days. Avoid using an infra-red heater for ducklings. They are messy in their drinking habits, and there is a good chance that they will cause the lamps to blow by splashing water on them. It is far better to use the dull emitters, as they are more robust and will not shatter.

Follow the basic programme suggested for chickens and bantams until, *provided that* weather conditions are normal for the time of year, you should be able to dispense with artificial heat by the end of that time. After a week indoors without heat, the young birds can be transferred to an outdoor coop and run, which is best constructed with wire mesh in a suitable corner of the garden.

For birds supposedly at home in an aquatic environment, it is surprising to discover that water causes potential problems in some aspects of duck rearing. The chosen drinker for ducklings must not be too deep, as they are notorious for 'playing' in water and, in doing so, suffering from chilling. If a narrow-based fountain is unobtainable, pebbles, a length of hose or even marbles placed around the base will prevent full access, and should go a long way towards preventing any deaths. For the same reasons, it is important to protect the ducklings from rain until their mature feathers

Duckling brooding box.

develop, at about three months. At the other end of the meteorological scale, young ducklings can suffer quite badly from sunstroke, and great care must be taken when they are first placed outdoors.

Artificially reared ducklings will appreciate the addition of fresh greens to their diet and small quantities of freshly cut grass or chopped dandelions are ideal.

Geese

Provided that the area contains short-cropped grass, and there are not too many obstacles in or behind which young goslings can get trapped, there should be no problem in leaving a mother goose in her own environment once her clutch has hatched. Any other geese tend to become doting 'aunts' and the gander is usually a proud, protective and attentive father.

Artificially hatched goslings can be reared in much the same way as ducklings and once again infra-red lamps are a convenient source of heat for brooding small numbers of birds. The most commonly used is the 250-watt brooder lamp, which will easily keep up to thirty goslings warm. If using hover-type brooders, brood only a quarter as many goslings as the manufacturer's chick capacity states. Because goslings are larger than chicks, it may also be necessary to start off with them at a higher level, reducing the heat by 5 to 10° per week. Be aware of the fact that too high a temperature may well result in slower feathering and growth. Observe the birds: if they stay away from the heat, turn it down or off.

As they grow, the goslings will obviously need more space. If they get their pen messy rapidly, they need more bedding and more space. By the age of five or six weeks they can probably be outside all the time, except in extremely cold, wet weather. Make sure that the forecast is good before putting them outside for the first time.

Turkeys

Young turkeys hatched and reared by their natural mothers fare much better if the hen has an enclosure rather than being confined to a coop. Those that are reared in this way are much hardier than those that have been cooped and purely artificially fed. They are also less susceptible to sudden showers of rain, because the natural preening instinct and feather oils develop more quickly. With fine weather the birds will thrive outside on grass and the exercise will certainly help them to develop fully.

Most birds for the Christmas market are bought in at day-old and so, unless you have a couple of broody chickens ready and awaiting their arrival, there is usually no alternative but to rear turkeys by artificial means. Again, the methods used are similar to those described for other varieties, but one important point to make is that turkeys raised outside could succumb to Blackhead disease (*see* Chapter 7). Although chickens are fairly resistant to the condition, turkeys are very susceptible.

Another point to be aware of is that, as they begin to develop, turkey poults may begin bullying and feather-pecking. Caught early enough, the wounds can be dusted with antibiotic powder and, once isolated, the victim will quickly recover. Stress and over-crowding can exacerbate this behaviour, but it may also be experienced in very small groups of birds that have plenty of space available.

Guinea-Fowl

Guinea-fowl chicks are, like their game-bird cousins, very lively and can escape through even the smallest gap. For this reason, small-mesh netting of 1cm ($^1/_2$ in) should be used when constructing a coop and run. Make sure that there are no holes around the base and, if there are, block them with a brick. Better still, cover the base of the run with netting so that the chicks (keets) still have access to the grass and insects but cannot scratch their way out.

When rearing guinea-fowl chicks by artificial means, most of what has already been mentioned with regards to other types of poultry applies, but do not forget that they are far more flighty: it is therefore essential that whatever method of brooding is used, they are prevented from escaping by fitting a secure netting or wire-covered top.

Being members of the game-bird family, overcrowded or bored chicks may be prone to feather-pecking and it is important to have plenty of containers so that there is no competition for feed. (The same applies to drinkers.) It is also a good idea to provide additional attractions to keep the bird occupied, such as greenstuffs hung up for them to peck at.

Quail

A small bantam hen will normally incubate and successfully hatch all the fertile quail eggs placed under her. She will help feed the chicks and brood them brilliantly after they are hatched.

If the chicks are hatched by means of an incubator, once they are dry, they can be placed in a cardboard box to act as a brooder, using a 60-watt red electric light bulb to provide heat, hung approximately 100mm (4in) above the floor. The lamp must be adjustable up and down to provide the correct brooding temperature; the chicks will huddle together if they are cold or will move to the corners if too hot. Corrugated cardboard on the floor will stop the chicks slipping – it is best not to use newspaper, as this can induce 'splayed' legs in such tiny birds. Remember that quail chicks can fly soon after they hatch, so the brooder should be covered with fine netting to prevent escapees. A few days after hatching, the chicks should be moved into a more permanent heated cage. As the chicks grow, the heat can be reduced each week, until, at around four weeks, they will be fully feathered and not require warmth.

Once the young quail have matured, you need to keep a close watch on them, as the males will start to fight over the females, and feather-pecking could break out. Splitting the males from the females may help in reducing potential conflict. Select the best birds for breeding and/or egg laying and keep the surplus to mature as table birds.

— 7 —

Health and Hygiene

Provided that they are cared for sensibly, backyard poultry are unlikely to suffer from the sort of health problems that periodically beset commercial poultry farmers. Having said that, the fact that most small flocks are kept with access to the open air means that they could be more vulnerable to certain air-borne diseases with which intensively reared birds cannot come into contact.

Although it is necessary to be aware of potential problems, you should be wary of always thinking the worst. One of the symptoms of anatipestifer infection (duck septicaemia), for example, is watery eyes and nostrils, but 'weepy' eyes are much more likely to be a result of a hot, dry summer. Likewise, there are a number of possible reasons for lameness in chickens and bantams, and an injured leg is more likely to be the result of a bird dropping wrongly from the perch or pop-hole ramp than a symptom of a potentially serious disease such as Marek's.

Nevertheless, it would be foolish to assume that nothing can go wrong, even in a backyard situation, so it pays never to cut corners with general hygiene and the daily routine.

ROUTINE HYGIENE

Issues of hygiene are mostly a matter of common sense – if poultry houses are clean, light and well ventilated, and the floor is covered with litter that is regularly changed, there should be few or no hygiene problems. Inevitably, dark areas, dust, faeces and damp bedding will harbour problems and must be avoided at all costs.

The daily routine should include a number of activities: the dropping board fitted under most chicken and bantam house perches should be scraped; soiled bedding in the night shelters of ducks and geese should be removed; and any wet areas around feeders and drinkers must be replaced with dry litter. Nest-box material should be changed once a week, or straight away if an egg

Faeces and damp and dirty bedding will encourage problems and must be avoided.

has been accidentally broken. Depending on the type of housing used, it might be necessary to replace the floor covering completely on a monthly basis. In any case, it is essential to strip the house completely of all furnishings such as perches and nesting boxes at least once (and preferably twice) a year, in order to disinfect everything. Choose a dry, sunny day to carry out this operation so that the interior of the shed will be dry and aired before its inhabitants return for the night.

Hoppers and drinkers will benefit from a daily brush-out before being refilled with fresh food and water. With the exception of ducks and geese, if all other types of fowl are kept outside but housed overnight, and can readily go into the house whenever they wish, it is a good idea to keep their drinking water inside. This way, it is less likely to be contaminated by wild-bird droppings; also, it will be in the shade and remain cooler.

The shed where the food is kept should be cool, dry and well ventilated. Food must also be protected from dirt, dust and vermin. Any sacks or bags containing feed must never be placed directly on to a stone or concrete floor. No matter how dry it appears to you, condensation and moisture will undoubtedly build up between the floor and bag; that is why agricultural merchants keep their food stored on pallets or shelving. It is also a mistake to use any manu-factured rations that have gone over their expiry date – not only is there always the danger that the food itself may have 'gone off', it is also a fair assumption that any beneficial drugs or vitamins con-tained in it will be far less efficacious, or even totally ineffective. If, for whatever reason, any food becomes damp or spoilt, it should be immediately discarded.

As long as there is no danger of the chemicals being accessible to family pets, it is a good idea to keep several baiting points continu-ously supplied with rat and mouse poison. This is especially impor-tant in small gardens, where there are likely to be neighbours and you need to take immediate care of vermin for both social and hygienic reasons. It is possible to buy poisons in plastic sachets and these are, undeniably, the best option, as they keep the contents fresh until being chewed by rodents.

Keep all breeding and rearing pens clean, tidy and free from vermin.

AVIAN INFLUENZA

Avian influenza, or bird flu, has been around in its various forms for generations; it comes and goes and will continue to do so. It has been detected in the UK at least four times during the last 100 years; the main difference today is the fact that modern communications have made an outbreak more susceptible to media hyperbole – a situation more potentially devastating and damaging than the disease itself.

There has been much discussion on the subject of disease and its effect on the poultry world since the most recent discovery of avian flu. Although it is undoubtedly a serious subject, and avian influenza is one of two notifiable diseases (the other being Newcastle disease or fowl pest), there should be no need to worry on a day-to-day basis – provided you are vigilant regarding the health of your birds.

In the event of a serious outbreak, it would be a legal requirement to house all poultry and birds, including ducks, geese, captive wildfowl, raptors and game birds. This applies whether they are kept on a commercial basis or as a hobby. If housing was too difficult, there would be no alternative but to consider culling at least some of the birds. Flocks containing more than 50 birds must be registered with DEFRA, so that they know the whereabouts of all types of poultry within a given area and, therefore, would be better able to monitor any outbreak situation. There have also been significant advances in the creation of vaccines since the early part of 2006 and the approval of new vaccines provides the government, as well as producers, with additional 'tools' to counter the threat of disease. (*Poulvac Flufend i A1 H5N9* has already been purchased by many European governments to create 'vaccine banks'.)

At the time of writing (spring 2007), DEFRA and the Poultry Club of Great Britain recommend adopting the following policy:

- Keep feed under cover to minimize wild bird attraction.
- Keep water fresh and free of droppings.
- Keep waterfowl and chickens separate.
- Control vermin.
- Quarantine new stock for 2–3 weeks and birds that have been to a show or exhibition for seven days.
- Change clothes and wash boots before and after visiting other breeders or attending a show or sale.
- Keep disinfectant footbaths at the entrance to areas where poultry are kept.
- Disinfect crates before and after use, especially if lent to others. It is, however, preferable not to share equipment.

- Comply with any import/export regulations or DEFRA guidelines.

SOME COMMON PROBLEMS

A description of all the diseases that might affect poultry would be inappropriate in this book – many of the more serious problems occur only in situations of mass production and will very rarely trouble the backyard poultry keeper. However, you should have some knowledge of the more common general problems that may be encountered.

Worms

Even on virgin pasture there are small amounts of intestinal worms awaiting a host that will allow them to develop and proliferate. Poultry reared and kept intensively will rarely have a problem with worms, but, in all other circumstances, it is wise to carry out a regular worming programme at least twice a year.

The comprehensive range of poultry medications readily available on the market makes the treatment of minor ailments a relatively simple matter.

Roundworms are the most common. They produce eggs, which are laid in the bird's intestines and pass out through the faeces, being seen as tiny round balls sticking to solid droppings. These eggs fall on the ground and undergo a period of maturation, after which they are picked up by other birds and eventually develop in their intestines.

Although in some cases the eggs of *tapeworms* pass out through the droppings, it is more common for segments containing eggs of the worm to break off. After being secreted, they are eaten by slugs, snails and beetles where they hatch out in their interim host before being re-digested by the birds as they forage.

Hairworms develop and live in the blind gut (caeca) and are generally found in flocks that have been over-stocked. The worm is so small that it cannot be easily seen – probably the best way of finding evidence is to mix faeces with water, and then to detect the fine hairworms once they have been separated from all other matter.

Gapeworms normally make use of game birds as their host, but, where there is an over-population of game running over the same land, then your poultry will almost inevitably become the host medium. The most obvious symptom of gapeworms is the bird reaching skywards with its neck, gasping for breath. The gapeworm lives in the windpipe (trachea) and, as it multiplies, partially blocks the airway. In a really bad individual case, temporary assistance can be given: oil a primary or secondary wing feather, hold the bird securely with its neck outstretched, then gently twist the feather and guide it down the bird's throat. Keep twisting as the feather is withdrawn and it should be possible to see a few gapeworms attached.

Although it is nowadays only available on prescription from the vet, or supplied by a supplier or feed manufacturer who has full knowledge of its use, 'Flubenvet' mixed in the rations and administered over a seven-day period is probably the best and certainly the easiest way to eradicate all parasitical worms.

Blackhead

Although chickens and bantams are fairly resistant, there is the distinct possibility that turkeys raised outside will succumb to blackhead. It is a protozoan parasite that is ingested in the ova of either *Heterakis* worms or as larvae in earthworms or faeces; it then attacks the liver. Symptoms of birds with blackhead are bright sulphur-yellow diarrhoea and, possibly, loss of weight or appetite, signs of depression and drooping wings.

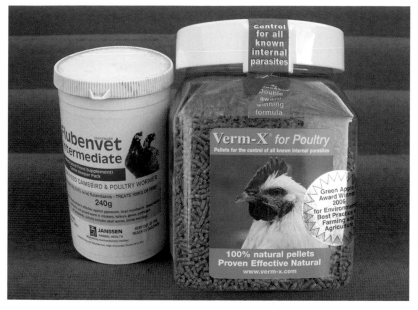

Examples of proprietary wormers.

The only known drug to cure blackhead is Dimetridazole, but its use was forbidden by EU legislation in 2004. The best advice that can be given is to carry out a strict hygiene and regular worming routine. If worming is done every six weeks, the life-cycle of the worm is disrupted before any damage to the liver can be done. Some turkey owners add a little cider vinegar to the drinking water, which is very effective in altering the gut's pH balance and therefore makes it more difficult for the worm to survive.

Parasites

When large numbers of *lice* are active on a bird, the most obvious signs are greyish-white eggs around the base of the vent feathers. In really bad cases they will also be seen around the 'armpit' area, under the wings. The lice are about the size of a pinhead and light brown in colour. Infestations are usually worse in the spring and summer months, causing irritation to adults and, sometimes, severe anaemia in young birds. Fortunately they are one of the easiest parasites to get rid of and, once discovered, can be eradicated by a proprietary louse powder purchased from agricultural suppliers.

If possible, spray and treat the poultry unit in the spring and autumn, making sure that all cracks and crevices are thoroughly coated. Use powder in the sheds, nest boxes, ends of perches and on the birds themselves. Before using any product, check that it is safe to use in your particular situation; if there is any doubt at all, try and speak to the manufacturer or supplier, or an experienced backyard poultry keeper, who should be able to advise on the best that is available. It is possible that some of the powders will not be licensed for use on poultry, but they are nevertheless excellent – the fact that a treatment is not licensed is often due to the cost of getting it registered rather than it being unsuitable or ineffective.

Northern mite can cause a huge amount of damage before being noticed. Similar in size to the red mite, they are normally grey to black in colour, but can show as red if they have just gorged on blood. Infected laying birds should be dusted with a pyrethrum-based powder rather than one which contains an avermectin, because the eggs are entering the food chain. Whatever product is chosen, northern mite is notoriously difficult to eradicate and repeated treatment will probably be necessary.

Unlike northern mite, which live on their host all the time, red mite live and breed in crevices found in the house and only 'hop' on

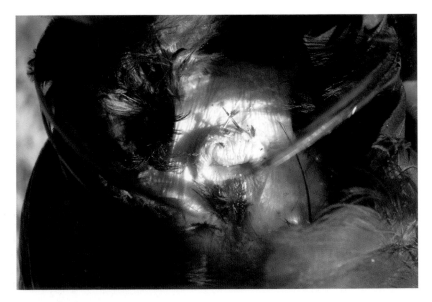

An example of a northern mite infestation around the vent area (on the sparse feathering, centre of picture).

to the bird for a quick meal. It is pointless looking for them on the birds: they will be more readily seen by inspecting the perches and nest boxes. Red mite can live for many months without feeding, and have been known to lie dormant for several years. Despite their name, red mites are grey in colour and only appear red after feeding. Red spots on the shells of eggs are almost certainly red mite droppings. Houses should be sprayed with 'Barricade' or a similar product such as 'Crusade', which is available in pet shops and is useful for the smaller hen house or coop and run.

Depluming or *feather mites* live at the base of the feathers and attack the feather shafts. In really severe cases they can cause the feathers to fall out, or may irritate the bird so badly that it begins to pull out its own feathers. The symptoms are sometimes mistaken for feather-pecking, especially as they tend to occur around the head and neck. Difficult to eradicate, they are best treated in the same way as northern and red mites.

Scaly leg mites burrow under the leg and foot scales and, in very bad cases, cause the scales to lift and peel. A treatment of 'Vaseline' not only blocks off the supply of oxygen to the mite, but also helps to loosen old scales and strengthen the new ones as they grow. Applied in a seven-day cycle, it kills and heals at the same time. An

The presence of scaly leg mites is often indicated by loose scales and a swollen appearance to the legs.

alternative would be benzyl benzoate, which can be bought from the chemist. Feather-legged types of chickens and bantams are particularly susceptible to scaly leg and, as it is more difficult to spot in amongst the feathers, owners of such breeds need to be more vigilant.

Poultry fleas tend to live in the dust of nest boxes and floors. The female fleas often lay their eggs in dirty nest box litter; these hatch in a week and mature in a month. Although they do not actually live on the birds, they can irritate them by biting. A proprietary flea powder will clear the problem on poultry but they will quickly become re-infected unless the house is cleaned and disinfected. *Hen fleas* have a slightly different life-cycle and live in the downy parts of the bird's feather. They are orange in colour, and can be confused with red mite.

Prolapse

A prolapse is more likely to be seen in a young underdeveloped bird that has just begun laying than it is in older stock. The vent tissues are evacuated along with an egg, which sometimes can be seen from the outside but is more likely to remain just inside the bird. If the egg can be seen, it might be possible to remove it (if necessary, gently break the shell) and clean the protruding tissue with a mild disinfectant before attempting to push the tissue back inside the bird. Keep the bird separate from the remainder of the flock for a few days and give it a plentiful supply of food and water. Occasionally, the tissue may exude again but it is well worth a second attempt at replacing it.

If a female is seen looking uncomfortable and hunched up, it could be that she is suffering from an egg blockage rather than a prolapse. When an egg is lodged in the cloaca, either because it is large or misshapen, the hen is said to be egg-bound. The bird may eventually lay the egg if she is kept isolated and away from the attentions of the rest of the flock. If she is an important part of your breeding programme or of quality show stock, it may pay to have her examined by a specialist poultry vet.

Egg Peritonitis

Egg peritonitis is caused by the yolk missing the infundibulum and falling into the abdominal cavity. The body then begins to reject it and infection occurs. Typical symptoms include lethargy and a penguin-like stance. There is no cure for the problem and it is kinder to kill the bird rather than allowing it to suffer for any length of time.

Feather-Pecking

If you have a particularly small garden and, despite all the advice given to the contrary, stock is overcrowded, feather-pecking may become a problem. Some types of poultry are more prone to this vice than others: ducks and geese very rarely succumb, chickens and bantams occasionally do, but it can be a big problem with turkeys and game birds (including guinea-fowl).

As birds develop, they can show natural pecking-order instincts and possible mating preparation behaviour, which is often exacerbated by overcrowded conditions. Usually seen as bullying and/or feather-pecking, it is a habit that, once started, is very difficult to stop. Even the smallest speck of blood attracts the attentions of other members of the flock and a bird that has been set on can suffer with a badly pecked head, wing feathers or vent; it may even eventually be killed if it is not removed from the flock immediately.

Clean bedding, sufficient light, appropriate levels of stocking, plenty of feed containers so that there is no competition for feed, enough drinkers and additional attractions (such as greenstuffs

When trimming the beak to prevent feather-pecking, it is important only to remove the very tip of the upper mandible.

hung up for them to peck at) to keep the birds occupied are all measures that will help. However, feather-pecking may still occur, even in very small groups that are housed in ideal conditions and have plenty of run space available.

The only solution in such a situation may be to consider debeaking or trimming, but it should only be done by someone experienced enough to know just how far back to trim. Only the tip of the upper mandible should be cut.

Egg-Eating

Egg-eating is rarely a problem with ducks and geese or free-range guinea-fowl, but chickens, bantams and turkeys will eat broken eggs if they find them, and may develop a taste for them. Normally, birds of any description do not consider unbroken eggs to be edible, but if the shell has something such as a leaf or speck of dirt attached to it, they will sometimes peck at it out of curiosity. If the shell then gets broken as a result, they will eagerly eat the contents.

To prevent egg-eating, provide nest boxes that are dark and make sure that there are enough of them for the number of birds expected to use them. Make them large enough so that a particularly clumsy

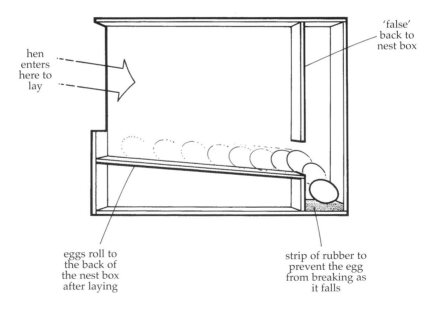

'false' back to nest box

hen enters here to lay

eggs roll to the back of the nest box after laying

strip of rubber to prevent the egg from breaking as it falls

A 'roll-away' nest box will prevent eggs from being pecked and eaten.

hen is unlikely to break any eggs laid earlier as she enters the box to lay her own. If necessary, make the box large but the opening small so that others cannot enter when one bird is still laying.

Should egg-eating become a problem, blown eggs filled with an unpleasant substance such as mustard is often given as a solution, but, as chickens do not have a particularly good sense of taste, this well-known remedy is unlikely to work. As a last resort, use 'roll-away' nest boxes – these can be bought, but you can also make them yourself by providing a box with a double bottom, the top one of which slopes towards the back, leaving a gap at the foot of the back wall. The newly laid egg will roll towards the back of the box before dropping on to the second lower bottom, which should be covered with soft material so that the egg is not damaged as it falls.

USING ANTIBIOTICS

It is important to be wary of giving antibiotics unless a problem has been specifically diagnosed, as it could merely have the effect of masking a serious disease. It is essential to know exactly what the problem is: for example, mycoplasma (a respiratory disease, with symptoms of sneezing, discharge from the eyes and nostrils and, most prominently, a swollen sinus on one or both sides of the head) is not a bacterium but is in a class of its own. The only effective antibiotic in such a situation would be Tylan, which is licensed (in soluble form) for poultry. The soluble works well with young stock but is not so good with adult birds, which would benefit more from an injection of Tylan 200. It should not be given to poultry being produced for meat, however, as its 'carrier' can harm muscle. In egg producers or show birds, vets may recommend its use even though it is not licensed for poultry.

There are occasions when, if one antibiotic does not appear to be working, it may be worth trying another family of antibiotics, as the causal bacteria may not be susceptible to the first.

THE MOULT

During the first year of life, it is unusual for poultry to moult once they have grown their adult feathers, although giving young birds layer's pellets too early on can result in a partial or neck moult. At the end of the second summer, most, particularly chickens, bantams and turkeys, will go into a moult and lose the majority of their feathers. During this period, laying hens will produce fewer eggs or, more usually, stop completely. It is important that they receive good nutrition at this time so that their bodies are given the chance to 'recharge their batteries' and build up the necessary reserves of nutrients.

There are, however, certain factors other than the annual ones imposed by Mother Nature that may induce what might best be termed as 'un-natural' moulting. A lack of feathers on the neck and nape may be due to the unwanted attentions of other birds in the flock; it might also be that plucked, broken or otherwise missing feathers on the back and neck of females are simply due to over-vigorous attention from the male bird during mating. Other, more serious causes include the following:

- decreasing daylight or artificial light;
- loss of body weight;
- disease;
- internal parasites;
- infestation of the depluming mite (*see* page 113);
- extremes of weather – excessive cold or a heatwave;
- feed, feeding and feedstuffs: deficiencies of essential ingredients; insufficient or irregular feeding;
- predators such as foxes, cats and dogs;
- position in the pecking order, resulting in low vitality and a sullen, miserable appearance;
- prolonged broodiness;
- general human-induced stress, including exposed housing, overcrowding, movement to another house, water deprivation and/or insufficient water space, faulty ventilation, wet litter.

Longevity

As a general rule, lighter breeds tend to live longer than the heavier types, but individual birds will often prove this table wrong.

Geese: 10–20 years
Large fowl, turkeys and guinea-fowl: 6–10 years
Bantams and peafowl: 8–12 years
Ducks: 6–8 years
Quail: 1–2 years

— 8 —

Eggs and Meat

Even if you have no intention to sell eggs and table birds, your hobby will, on occasion, result in some surplus stock. Hopefully, 'spare' birds can be sold to other fanciers, but, whilst the females of any species will probably find a good home quite quickly, it is unlikely that you will be able to off-load more than the odd cockerel, drake, gander or stag. You will be faced with no alternative but to cull them, and it is surely pointless simply killing them and burying them in the garden. If you can harden your heart and bring yourself to do so, it is worth taking the trouble to prepare them for the table. In the case of a young bird, plucking is a lot of bother for what amounts to a few mouthfuls on the dinner plate, but there is no need to go to such extremes – all you really need to do is cut off the breast meat, stick it in the freezer and then use it in a stir-fry later on.

An excess of eggs might cause a problem, especially when the flock is in full lay in the spring and early summer. If you have more than you know what to do with – and relatives and neighbours hide behind closed doors when they see you approaching with yet another egg box – you might need to try some lateral thinking and use the surplus in recipes for the freezer. Alternatively, try the old stand-by of pickling. Do not think of starting a regular egg round when you have a seasonal glut, because, once things get back to normal, you will not have enough to supply your regular customers – unless you go out and buy more layers, which is rather defeating the object!

If space, time and circumstances allow you the opportunity to sell produce on a regular basis, marketing should be arranged well in advance of production, and at the appropriate time to maximize profits. Being stuck with unsold perishable 'goods' will obviously result in a loss. The successful producer has a good knowledge of certain subjects: how to research the potential market; how to choose stock wisely; a clear understanding of time scales; and a familiarity with the rules and regulations relating to the sale of table birds and eggs.

CHICKENS AND BANTAMS

The size of a chicken's egg will be determined by the species, breed and age of the bird; pullets will produce smaller eggs than a mature hen when they first begin laying and should come into lay at around five to six months of age. They will continue to lay well for the following year, after which time their annual production will gradually lessen.

If your free-range birds take to laying outside rather than in the nest boxes provided, much potential profit will be lost, so do not let them out of their house and/or run until mid-morning, by which time most should have finished laying. In an effort to prevent any broken eggs, keep nest boxes full of fresh, clean litter; collect eggs frequently; provide sufficient nest boxes; and feed the correct ration – deficiencies can lead to thin-shelled eggs, which are more likely to get broken.

Commercial meat-producing birds will obviously give a heavier weight more quickly than some of the more traditional breeds. If you prefer to keep the more traditional types, why not capitalize on their breeding and make much of the fact that they have been reared free-range in your 'marketing' strategy?

Dirty nests will result in dirty and broken eggs. Regular cleaning and replenishing of suitable litter material is essential.

DUCKS

Breeds such as the Khaki Campbell are known to lay as many as 300 eggs in a single season. Like chickens, ducks tend to lay most of their eggs in the early morning and, if given free-range, will lay in vegetation and then cover their eggs with grass, making them difficult, if not impossible, to find. To avoid such problems, it is better to keep ducks confined in their house until about 10am.

Ducks intended for the table should be marketed at around ten weeks. Keeping them beyond this time may result in a loss of condition and, from a practical point of view, they will undoubtedly be more of a problem to pluck, due to the new stubbly feather growth.

GEESE

Goose eggs contain a vast amount of yolk and are therefore very rich and something of an acquired taste. They do not, unlike some other types of poultry, lay for most of the year and their breeding season is short. Eggs are laid from about February to late May, with laying being triggered by the lengthening days. Each goose

A plate of prize-winning duck eggs.

121

will lay about twenty eggs; if their eggs are not removed from the nest, they will usually stop after about twelve, and sometimes less, depending on the breed. A large goose egg is about the weight of three hen's eggs and makes wonderful scrambled egg and omelettes.

Goose as a meat is at its best in the first year. It is a moist, very tasty meat with its own individual and unique taste. Once geese begin to mate or lay, however, the quality of the flesh toughens and never really regains its delicacy. Breed birds in the spring for marketing at the end of the same year.

TURKEYS

Although turkeys obviously do lay eggs, the bird is normally kept to produce youngsters to provide a meat carcass, and most eggs are held back for breeding purposes. If you have eggs to spare, it is very unlikely that you will find many purchasers beating a path to your door. It makes more sense to sell any surplus eggs as fertile (for which you will obviously need a stag or 'tom'), and concentrate on breeding chicks (poults) or buying in day-olds for the oven-ready market.

Once killed, the carcasses should, if the weather is not too warm or you have access to a chiller or cold store, be hung for about ten days before evisceration. This tenderizes the meat and improves the flavour in the same way as the traditional method of hanging game birds. Remember to hang them well away from anything that could contaminate the flesh.

QUAIL

Laying quail kept together do not generally bother about nests, preferring to lay anywhere in the floor litter. Egg production increases if there are no males present. Apart from using fresh eggs for hard-boiling as a picnic treat, another possibility is to hard-boil them and place them in aspic or pickle them in vinegar and salt; they can also be smoked. The shell will dissolve completely if the boiled egg is placed in commercial vinegar for twelve hours or it can be hand-peeled.

Quail meat is, like revenge, a dish best served cold! For a dinner party you would probably need two birds per person, but as an accompaniment to a summer salad or picnic, it cannot be bettered.

GUINEA-FOWL

Despite the fact that guinea-fowl will lay a considerable number of eggs, the seasonality of production means that the egg market is not a viable option. Instead, it is meat production that is likely to be of most interest.

The flesh of a guinea-fowl is game-like in flavour, colour and texture, and its dark colour alone may be enough to deter the would-be purchaser. Selling to restaurants might be your best option – it seems that the British public are more likely to try something 'exotic' on a menu than they are to buy a bird, find a recipe and cook it themselves!

EGG PRODUCTION

Numbers

The number of eggs a bird lays is dependent on the time of year, its breed and age, the quality of food supplied and the conditions in which the birds are kept. Most of the commercially bred chickens that have been selected over generations purely as layers will produce anywhere between 200 and 320 eggs during their first proper season. After this, numbers will gradually decrease as the bird gets older. If eggs are the main reason for keeping poultry, it is obviously a mistake to choose a breed that has been bred for table or exhibition purposes, as these will lay well only in the spring and early summer.

One chicken can only lay, at the most, seven eggs a week, while most lay fewer. If you are intent on creating an egg round or selling eggs to outlets on a regular basis, it is important to bear this fact in mind. Similarly, you need to remember that egg productivity diminishes annually and that, after three or four years, laying will become more spasmodic. You might wish to consider the option of culling birds after their second proper season of laying if eggs are the be-all and end-all of your venture.

Storage

Eggs left in nests risk getting re-warmed or damaged when the nest is occupied by another bird, so it is important to collect them as often as is conveniently possible. Once they have been collected, they should, ideally, be in a controlled cool environment within thirty

A handful of freshly collected eggs.

minutes. As the egg cools its contents contract and any bacteria on the shell will be drawn into the egg through its pores.

All eggs are porous and, with all types of poultry, it is essential that any dirty eggs are cleaned immediately after collection in order to prevent bacteria entering via the shell. It is a simple matter to rub off the odd specks of dirt on a very lightly soiled egg, but a bucketful of muddy duck eggs is a more difficult proposition. Cleaning eggs with sandpaper, wire wool or a knife will have a negative effect by grinding the bacteria into the egg.

It is possible to buy proprietary solutions that will clean off the egg surface and also kill off any harmful bacteria. Each manufacturer has their own product and it is important to adhere to the particular instructions.

When a shell is dry, bacteria are less likely to enter the egg, since they much prefer a wet surface. If numbers do not justify the use of a 'proper' egg wash, make sure that any odd eggs that need to be cleaned by hand are washed in water that is warmer than the egg, and then dried well with a piece of kitchen paper.

Eggs should be stored in a constant temperature so the shed where you keep them must be either insulated or cooled until the temperature of the egg is 15–20°C (59–68°F). It is also important to avoid the possibility of any sort of contamination by not keeping a mixture of items (feedstuffs, for example) in the same building, or at least in the immediate area chosen for storage. Condensation on shells can increase the risk of bacteria, so try to avoid its build-up by not taking cooled eggs into humid conditions or allowing warm air into the storage area.

Keep eggs on clean trays (remembering that papier-mâché trays will retain an un-cooled egg's heat for several hours), situated well away from walls and ceilings, in order to ensure good air circulation. Finally, clearly mark or label batches of eggs with dates and any other relevant information. Eggs for sale must be date-stamped, and this can done with a small hand-held stamp.

PREPARING A BIRD FOR THE TABLE

Killing

All birds should be starved for twenty-four hours prior to killing, as this allows time for them to empty themselves fully, which makes the task of preparation easier and cleaner. They must, however, be given water during this time.

To kill a chicken, bantam, guinea-fowl or quail is relatively easy once the basics are understood. A quail can be dispatched by simply pressing a thumb into the back of the head, but the more usual method for the others is to dislocate the neck. This is best achieved by holding the bird's legs in one hand (usually your weaker hand), taking the neck and hackle area in the other, and then pulling the head down and twisting it backwards simultaneously.

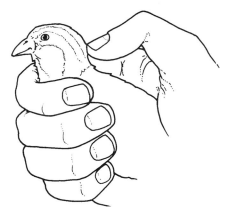

Quail can be easily dispatched by pressing a thumb into the back of the bird's head.

125

The most usual method for ducks, geese and turkeys is to lay their head on the ground (chin on ground, beak facing forward) while holding their feet, so that you are looking at their back. Place a broom handle over the neck and hold it firmly in place with your feet (one either side of the bird), then pull upwards on the legs with both hands; this dislocates the neck in the same way as for the smaller types of fowl.

The head may, unfortunately, become completely detached if you are too vigorous; although this is unpleasant and messy, the bird will not suffer. With or without its head, the bird may go into violent spasms and flap its wings for some seconds after the deed is done; this is nothing to worry about, as it is simply a reaction of the nervous system.

Once it has been killed, the bird should be plucked straight away. It makes the job easier and you will have a more professional end result if the feathers are removed while the carcass is still warm.

Plucking

Big birds such as turkeys and geese can be plucked with the carcass suspended from a rafter in a shed, but for others, it is perhaps easier to sit on a box and position the bird comfortably across both

A broomstick may be the preferred method of dislocating the neck of a larger bird.

Other Methods

The Humane Slaughter Association (HSA) advises that the aim of any slaughter method should be to render a bird unconscious and to quickly induce death thereafter. They point out that neck dislocation without prior stunning is legal provided that death is achieved without pain or suffering.

• Mechanical devices developed to produce a concussive blow (mainly found in commercial establishments) must, under current legislation, be followed by neck cutting or neck dislocation. Likewise, electric stunning must be followed up by a similar action.

• Decapitation without prior stunning is legal, but again not recommended due to the fact that brain activity may continue for up to 30 seconds.

For further information, email: info@hsa.org.uk or visit www.hsa.org.uk

knees. Cover yourself with a sack or, better still, wear overalls, as the fine downy feathers of any bird are quite good at attaching themselves to woollen jumpers and human hair, and finding their way down your wellingtons!

The flight and tail feathers should be removed first before moving on to the breast, followed by the sides, back, legs and wings. Care should be taken in plucking the breast feathers, especially over the narrow feather tract areas – holding the skin tightly with one hand to prevent tearing, and pulling out small groups of feathers against the natural direction of their lie with the other, will minimize damage to the skin.

Wet plucking is normally only carried out in large commercial set-ups, but it can be a useful practice when it comes to dealing with ducks and geese, the feathers of which are much harder to remove by hand than are those of other types of poultry. Basically, the birds should be dipped into a bath of hot water heated to 49–54.5°C (120–130°F) for 15–30 seconds, depending upon the weight of the individual bird. Feathers can then be removed more easily, either by hand or with the aid of a plucking machine.

Plucking Machines

A plucking machine may prove a useful asset if you are hoping to produce table birds on a regular basis. There are several types available and their operation requires no special skill. Suction is developed at the plucking head, which in turn draws feathers into a set of rotating plates or rubber 'fingers', where they are gripped and pulled from the body. They are then channelled through a suction unit into a collection sack. The grip on the feathers can be adjusted to obtain optimum plucking times; in the case of guinea-fowl, this can be as little as a minute. Chickens normally take 3–4 minutes and a turkey or goose 5–10 minutes. A guard is fitted to prevent damage to the bird's skin and a single-phase machine can be plugged into a standard 13-amp socket.

Any stubbly feathers (caused by new growth on a young bird) can be removed once the bird has cooled and the skin has begun to set firm. To finish the job, singe off the body hairs with a cigarette lighter, lighted taper or over a gas flame.

Evisceration

Next, turn the bird on to its breast and slit the skin vertically from the back of the head down to the base of the neck in order to expose the vertebrae. It should be possible to identify the break that occurred at killing by the presence of a small cavity of congealed blood; cut the head off at this point and, feeling with your knife, cut through the neck at the place where it connects to the body. You should then be left with the neck as a separate piece to package along with the heart, gizzard and liver (*see* below) and, on the carcass itself, a flap of skin folding over from the front.

Break and twist the legs at the rounded joint where the scaly part of the leg attaches to the thigh (you may need to cut around the joint with a knife if you do not have this action exactly right), and pull the feet away from the body. With a little effort they should come clean away, hopefully bringing with them at least some of the sinews that run through the fleshy part of the thigh.

The internal organs, some of which you may wish to keep for stock (heart, gizzard and liver), are removed by making a small incision between the vent and just below the parson's nose. Cut

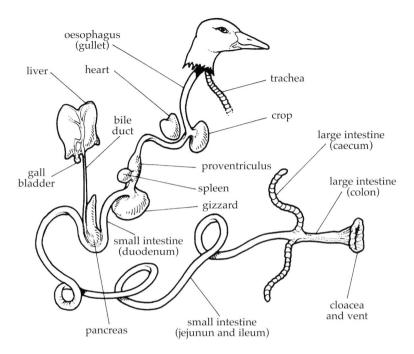

To keep the heart, gizzard and liver for later use, it is necessary to be able to identify them from the rest of the bird's intestines!

carefully around the rectum to detach it from the rest of the body. By inserting your hand (fingers in the case of guinea-fowl or quail) into the gap created, you should be able to remove most, if not all, of the internal organs in one operation. Once you have pulled everything out, wipe the insides with a clean damp tea towel or several sheets of kitchen paper.

If you want to keep the heart, gizzard and liver, separate them from the rest of the organs, which can then be discarded. The gizzard is easily identified by its blue/silver colour and muscled appearance; its insides should be cleaned by carefully cutting three-quarters of the way around its edges and opening it up like a book.

Finally, at the head end of the bird, feel inside the flap of skin that was created by removing the neck and pull out the crop. Also, check that the windpipe (trachea) came away when the neck was detached during earlier operations. You might like to truss the bird in order to give it a more professional appearance, but otherwise the bird is now ready for the oven.

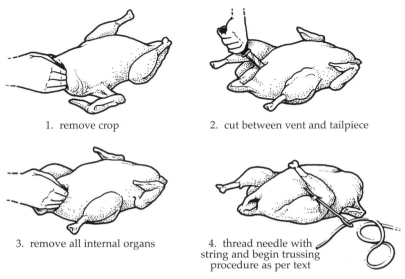

1. remove crop

2. cut between vent and tailpiece

3. remove all internal organs

4. thread needle with string and begin trussing procedure as per text

Trussing a bird gives it a more professional-looking finished appearance.

Trussing

To truss a bird, you need either an old-fashioned trussing needle or a large, wide-eyed darning needle. Place the bird on its back and press its thighs level with the table. Thread the needle with some thin clean white string and pass it through the folds of the legs and out the other side. Turn the carcass on to its breast and thread the needle through the closed wings. Pass the needle in the opposite direction through the other wing before untying the threaded needle and tying the two end pieces of string together. A more modern method is to use strong rubber-like bands, which hold the carcass together in exactly the same way.

SELLING TO THE PUBLIC

The Legalities

Although EU legislation does not apply to meat production for private use, there are certain hygiene regulations that must be adhered to if you intend to sell birds. You will need to notify the local authority of your intentions. An Environmental Health Officer will then inspect the premises and hopefully give approval for your plans. On a semi-commercial basis, it will probably be necessary to have approved plucking, eviscerating and packaging areas, which could be quite costly. In light of legislation that came into force in January 2006, would-be meat producers are advised to contact the Food Standards Agency (FSA) to ensure that they comply with any food regulations concerning hygiene, labelling and marketing.

There are also regulations relating to the disposal of the parts of the bird that are not intended for human consumption. The EU Animal By-Products Regulation 2003 requires that all offal should be disposed of via an approved knacker-man and the feathers, head and intestines certainly cannot be placed along with household rubbish destined for landfill.

On the subject of slaughter, rules are set down in Directive 93/119/EC, which is implemented in Great Britain by the Welfare of Animals (slaughter and killing) Regulations 1995. Schedule 1 of the Regulations stipulates the necessary licensing procedures for slaughtermen, but exempts from this schedule anyone who slaughters or kills any animal elsewhere than in a slaughterhouse or knacker's yard, *provided that he is the owner of the animal or bird and that it is for private consumption.*

Marketing

Selling eggs and meat directly to the customer has to be the best way of marketing, but there are also a number of opportunities for selling directly to caterers and shops, as long as you adhere to all the relevant legislation.

No matter what form your marketing takes, it is important to offer only a first-class quality product. Eggs must be clean and well packaged whilst table birds must be well dressed and presented. Customers are more likely to buy a tray of brown eggs than a tray of white, even though there is no nutritional difference. Likewise, consumers will accept poultry that is white or of a colour that is generally accepted as 'right' and will avoid a carcass containing excessive reddening and darkening of the meat, bruising or remains of feathers. In actual fact, a wholesome-looking pack may be positively dangerous if incorrectly stored, whereas a poor-looking pack may be of excellent quality. Nevertheless, it is essential to remember the old adage that 'the customer is always right' and to make every effort to give them what they want.

Customers will often ask if the meat or eggs you have on offer are free-range or organic and it is important to appreciate the difference between the two terms. Organically produced stock must be kept on

An egg-grading machine is usually only needed by large-scale poultry operations.

ground that has been free of artificial fertilizers and pesticides for several years, and the birds themselves must not have been subjected to growth hormone products or antibiotics. 'Free-range' poultry, on the other hand, may have been kept on any type of ground, given antibiotics and growth promoters, and fed non-organic food. Both 'organic' and 'free-range' birds must, however, have daily access to the outdoors and, other than at night for their own protection, must not kept confined to buildings.

Packaging

Successful and appropriate packaging is necessary to assist with the preservation of the product, protect it from physical damage, confine it so that it remains intact, and add visual appeal so that customers will wish to buy. Those with artistic flair will welcome the opportunity to create their own packaging, which will be the most appropriate to their own product and locality.

Eggs
It is important that all eggs offered for sale are fresh – never be tempted to sell any eggs that have been laid in a hedge by free-ranging stock, as it only takes one of them to be stale for you to lose a customer. Eggs should be packed in egg boxes and/or trays, which

Old-fashioned egg packing boxes still make good containers when transporting any kind of eggs over a long distance.

are supplied as the traditional papier-mâché or fibre variety, clear plastic or polystyrene. To locate suppliers of boxes suitable for all sizes of eggs (including quail), simply type 'egg boxes' into an Internet search engine.

Table Birds
There are three types of packaging that may be of interest to the small-scale table bird producer:

1 Over-wrapping: an expanded or rigid plastic tray is over-wrapped with a clear film of high-oxygen and low water vapour permeability. This method is the most popular, but relies on good refrigeration;
2 Bag wrapping: whole birds are packed on trays, which are then sealed in a clear bag. As with the over-wrapping method, the bag must be made of material capable of high-oxygen, low water vapour permeability;
3 Vacuum packing: the use of gas-impermeable plastics reduces evaporative losses, prevents further microbial contamination and reduces the proliferation of any microbes already present.

NB: In some meat-packaging situations, the addition of a special absorbent pad of tissue is required to take up extra moisture.

Useful Contacts

POULTRY MAGAZINES

Country Smallholding (Editor: Diane Cowgill): Fair Oak Close,
Exeter Airport Business Park, Clyst Honiton, Exeter EX5 2UL
Smallholder (Editor: Liz Wright): Hook House, Hook Road,
Wimblington, March, Cambridgeshire PE15 0QL
Fancy Fowl (Editor: Kevin Davis): TP Publications,
The Publishing House, Station Road, Framlingham, Suffolk IP13 9EE
Feathered World (Editor: Bob Batty): 5 Winckley Street, Preston,
Lancashire PR1 2AA
Practical Poultry Magazine (Editor: Chris Graham):
Kelsey Publishing Group, Cudham Tithe Barn, Berry's Hill,
Cudham, Kent TN16 3AG
Poultry World (Editor: Richard Allison), 2nd Floor,
Quadrant House, Sutton, Surrey SM2 5AS. Tel: 020 8652 4020

POULTRY CLUBS AND BREED SOCIETY CONTACTS

(Reproduced by kind permission of *Fancy Fowl* magazine)

The Ancona Club: Mr P. Smedley, Leckby House, Flaxton, York,
YO60 7QZ. Tel: 01904 468387
The Scottish Ancona Club: as above
The Araucana Club: S.M.C. Thurland, Tan Y Rhos, Babell, Flint,
CH8 8PY. Tel: 01352 720043
The Asian Hard-Feather Club: Julia Keeling, Ballashee, Starvey
Road, German, Isle of Man, IM4 2AJ. Tel: 01624 801 825
The Australorp Club: Ian and Louise Simpson, Chestnut Farm,
Normanton, Southwell, Nottinghamshire, NG25 0PR. Tel: 01636 814958
The Barnevelder Club: Mr G. Broadhurst, Little Acres, Chapel
Acres, Tern Hill, Market Drayton, East Yorkshire, TF9 3PY.
Tel: 01630 638 630
The British Belgian Bantam Club: J. and M. Templeman, 11 Fen
Road, Pointon, Sleaford, Lincolnshire, NG34 0LZ. Tel: 01529 240091

The British Waterfowl Association: Sue Schubert, PO Box 163, Oxted, Surrey, RH8 0WP. Tel: 01892 740212

The Brahma Club: Mrs L. Beere, Allendale, Walsall Road, Muckley Corner, Lichfield, Staffordshire, WS14 OBP. Tel: 01543 376096

The British Call Duck Club: Mrs Jen Maskell, Maes-y-Coed, Llanarth, Ceredigion, SA47 0RG. Tel: 01545 580425

The Call Duck Association: Graham Barnard, Ty Cwmdar, Cwrt-y-Cadno, Llanwrda, Carmarthenshire. Tel: 01558 650532

The Cochin Club: Miss Nina Morgan, 83 Roseland Road, Waunarlydd, Swansea, SA5 4ST. Tel: 01792 874 280

The Croad Langshan Club: Lyn Heigl, Stillwaters, Thursley Road, Churt, Farnham, Surrey, GU10 2LQ. Tel: 01428 602992

The Derbyshire Redcap Club: Mrs J.L. Woodroffe, 1 Alsop Moor Cottages, Alsop-en-le-Dale, Ashbourne, Derbyshire, DE6 1QS. Tel: 01335 310305

The Domestic Fowl Trust: Honeybourne, Evesham, Worcestershire, WR11 7QZ. Tel: 01386 833083

The Domestic Waterfowl Club: Mike Hatcher, 2 Limetree Cottage, Brightwalton, Newbury, Berkshire, RG20 7BZ. Tel: 01488 638014

The Dorking Club: Mrs V. Roberts, Heather Bank, Hillings Lane, Menston, Ilkley, West Yorkshire, LS29 6AU. Tel: 01943 872660

The Dutch Bantam Club: Mrs C.A. Compton, Devonia, Northbrook, Micheldever, Winchester, Hampshire, SO21 3AH. Tel: 01962 774476

The Faverolles Society: Mrs S. Bruton, Park House, Codsall Wood, South Staffordshire, WV8 1QR. Tel: 01902 843055

The Frizzle Society: Mr Rob Whittington, Malthouse, Malthouse Lane, Chale, Isle of Wight, Hampshire, PO38 2HX. Tel: 01983 551295

The Scottish Game Club: Mr J. Webster, Blairhill, Oakley, Fife, Scotland, EH13 9AJ. Tel: 01383 850239

The Goose Club: Mrs Denise Moss, Llwyn Coed, Gelli, Clynderwen, Carmarthenshire, SA66 7HW. Tel: 01437 563309

The Hamburgh Club: Mr P. Harrison, 60 Dean Head Summit, Littleborough, Lancashire, OL15 9LZ. Tel: 01706 377653

The Indian Game Club: Craig Gardner, North Thorn Farm Cottage, Ashwater, Beauworthy, Devon, EX21 5HE. Tel: 01409 211370

The Indian Runner Club: Mr P. Meatyard, Denham, Higher Back Way, Bruton, Somerset, BA10 0DW. Tel: 01749 812758

The Indian Runner Duck Association: Mr Richard Sadler, 14 Birchin Lane, Nantwich, Cheshire, CW5 6JT. Tel: 01270 623775

The Japanese Bantam Club: Terry and Lisa Crook, Rivermead, Costessy Lane, Drayton, Norwich, Norfolk, NR8 6HD. Tel: 01603 868373

The Leghorn Club: Ian Sissons, Sunbeam Cottage, Rye Road, Guestling, Hastings, East Sussex, TN35 4LL. Tel: 01424 815186

The Marans Club: Mr A. Heeks, 44 Poplar Drive, Alsager, Staffordshire, ST7 2RW. Tel: 01270 882189

Midland Old English Game Club: Mr D. Hackett, 227 Long Lane, Halesowen, Birmingham, West Midlands, B62 9JT. Tel: 01214 214618

The Minorca Club: Rob Walker, Orangeville, Spring Grove Lane, Oldwood, Tenbury Wells, Worcestershire, WR15 8TE. Tel: 01584 819429

The Modern Game Club: Ms Jennifer O'Sullivan, 42 Sussex Avenue, Ashford, Kent, TN24 6NB. Tel: 01303 813428

The New Hampshire Red Club: Mr B. Friel, 46 Shrewsbury Road, Worksop, Derbyshire, S80 2TU. Tel: 01909 482099

The Old English Game Bantam Club: Mr M. Woolway, 31 Pencefnarda Road, Penyrhoel, Gorseinon, West Glamorgan, SA4 4FY. Tel: 01792 894433

The Old English Game Club, Carlisle: Mr and Mrs J. Barry, 1 Mealo Cottages, Allonby, Maryport, Cumbria, CA15 6PB

The Orpington Club: Andrew Richardson, Black Lane Head Farm, Nateby, Preston, Lancashire, PR3 0LH. Tel: 01253 790468

The Buff Orpington Club: Mr P. Smedley, Leckby House, Flaxton, North Yorkshire, YO60 7QZ. Tel: 01904 468387

The Pekin Bantam Club: Mr D. Sill, Wards End Farm, Marsden, Huddersfield, West Yorkshire, HD7 6NJ. Tel: 01484 841008

The Scottish Pekin Bantam Club: Mr S. Currie, Alton Burn Farm, Tarbolton, Mauchline, Ayrshire, KA5 5NH. Tel: 01292 541203

The Plymouth Rock Club: Robin Ramus, The Lodge, Busbridge Lakes, Hambledon Road, Godalming, Surrey, GU8 4AY. Tel: 01483 421957

The Scottish Plymouth Rock Club: Mr A. Kirkpatrick, Strathmore, Beith Road, Glenganock, Strathclyde, KA14 3BX. Tel: 01904 468387

The Poland Club: Mr and Mrs T. Beebe, The Oaks, 84 Sutton Spring Wood, Temple Normanton, Chesterfield, Derbyshire, S42 5DT. Tel: 01246 854647

The Poultry Club of Great Britain: Mrs Ann Bachmet, South Lodge, Creeton Road, Swinstead, Grantham, Lincolnshire, NG33 4PG. Tel: 01476 550067

The Rhode Island Red Club: Norman Steer, Crossways, Kerries Road, South Brent, Devon, TQ10 9DE. Tel: 01364 73294

The Scottish Rhode Island Red Club: Mr J. Gardiner, 24 Biggar Road, Libberton, Carnwath, Strathclyde, ML11 8LX. Tel: 01555 840867

The Rare Breeds Survival Trust: National Agricultural Centre, Stoneleigh Park, Warwickshire, CV8 2LZ. Tel: 02476 696551

The Rare Poultry Society: Anne Merriman, 'Danby', The Causeway, Congresbury, Bristol, BS49 5DJ. Tel: 01934 833619

The **Rosecomb Bantam Club**: Mr S. Taylor, Ormerod House Farm, Flag Lane, Euxton, Chorley, Lancashire, PR7 6EZ. Tel: 01257 451575
The Scottish Rosecomb Club: Mr A. Robertson, Loanknowe Farm, Eccles, Kelso, Scotland, TD5 7QT. Tel: 01573 470333
The Scots Dumpy Club: Mrs T. Hamilton-Gould, Tower Fields, Tusmore Road, Soulden, Bicester, Oxfordshire, OX6 9HY. Tel: 01869 346554
The Scots Grey Club: Mr R. Innes, Huntsmans House, The Kennels, Blandford Road, Bere Regis, Dorset, BH20 7JH. Tel: 01929 471416
The Sebright Club: Steve Fuller, 1 Ridge Farm Cottages, Rowhook, Horsham, West Sussex, RH12 3QB. Tel: 01306 628369
The Silkie Club: Mrs S. Bowser, Nettleham Heath Farm, Nettleham, Lincoln, LN2 2LU. Tel: 01522 754096
The Sussex Club: Mr M. Raisey, Rosebarn Farm, Burlscombe, Tiverton, Devon, EX16 7JJ. Tel: 01823 672789
The Scottish Sussex Club: Mrs R. Aitken, Hillberry, Dunnotter, Stonehaven, Kincardinshire, Scotland, AB3 2XB. Tel: 01569 766775
Turkey Club UK: Mrs J. Houghton-Wallace, Cults Farmhouse, Whithorn, Newton Stewart, Scotland, DG8 8HA. Tel: 01988 600763
Utility Poultry Breeders Association: Graham Smith, Morville Heath, Bridgenorth, Shropshire, WV16 5NA. Tel: 01661 844961
The Welsummer Club: Mr G. Johnson, Lynbrooke, Sheriffhales, Shifnal, Shropshire, TF11 8QX. Tel: 01952 460274
The Wyandotte Club: Mr D. Alsop, 5 Hawthorne Close, Chinley, High Peak, Derbyshire, SK23 6DD. Tel: 01663 750708
The Black Wyandotte Club: Mr Alan Brooker, 50 Wellington Road, Sandhurst, Berkshire, GU47 9AY. Tel: 01344 774462
The Laced Wyandotte Club: Mrs L. Vernon Miller, Blackwell Grange, Blackwell, Shipston on Stour, Warwickshire, CV36 4PF. Tel: 01608 682357
The Partridge and Pencilled Wyandotte Club: Mr K. Newbury, 2 Montpellier, Quarndon, Derbyshire, DE22 5JW. Tel: 01332 553130
The White Wyandotte Club: Mrs D. Procter, Lyndene, 41B Church Street, Ribchester, Preston, Lancashire, PR3 3YE. Tel: 01254 878319

SUPPLIERS OF GUINEA-FOWL, TABLE BIRDS AND QUAIL

All Year Round Birds, 1 Humbie Livingston, Edinburgh, Midlothian, EH27 8DS. Tel: 07932963767
Cyril Bason, Bank House, Corvedale Road, Craven Arms, Shropshire, SY7 9NG. Tel: 01588 673204 *
Devonshire Traditional Breed Centre, Downes, Crediton, Devon, EX17 3PL. Tel: 01363 772430

Greenacres Farm, Newtown Road, Hainford, Norwich, Norfolk, NR10 3LZ. Tel: 01603 891092 *
Heritage Poultry, PO Box 193, Ormskirk, Lancashire, L40 8WY. Tel: 01704 840980
Nicky Gibbard, 2 Willow View, Timberscombe, Minehead, Somerset, TA24 7TH. Tel: 01643 841540
Pondhouse Poultry, Pond House, Beckford Close, Beckford, Gloucestershire, GL20 7AG. Tel: 01386 882383
S and T Poultry, 3 Windsor Drive, Wisbech, Cambridgeshire, PE13 3HJ. Tel: 01945 585618
  * indicates commercial producers of table poultry

EQUIPMENT SUPPLIERS

Flyte so Fancy, The Cottage, Pulham, Dorchester, Dorset, DT2 7DX. Tel: 01300 345229
Kintaline Poultry Centre, Benderloch, Oban, Argyll, Scotland, PA37 1QS
The Poultry Pen, Weirside Farm, Redbourne Road, Waddingham, Gainsborough, Lincolnshire, DN21 4TD. Tel: 01652 679001
Regency Poultry, The Oaks, 84 Sutton Spring Wood, Temple Normanton, Chesterfield, Derbyshire, S42 5DT. Tel: 01246 854647
Sussex Poultry Rearers, Greenfields Farm, Fontwell Avenue, Eastergate, Chichester, West Sussex, PO20 3RU. Tel: 01243 542815
Wells Poultry Housing & Equipment, The Bungalow, Windsor Road, Brynmawr, Gwent, NP23 4HJ

PROFESSIONAL PHOTOGRAPHER OF POULTRY

Robert (Rupert) Stephenson, 46 Barker Butts Lane, Coundon, Coventry, CV6 1DT. Tel: 07974 140255
(*see* his photos on www.rupert-fish.co.uk)

OTHER USEFUL ADDRESSES

British Poultry Council: Europoint House, 5 Lavington Street, London, SE1 0NZ. Tel: 020 7202 4760. www.poultry.uk.com
Food Standards Agency: 125 Kingsway, London, WC2B. Tel: 020 7276 8181. www.food.gov.uk
Humane Slaughter Association: The Old School, Brewhouse Hill, Wheathampstead, Hertfordshire, AL4 8AN. Tel: 01582 831919. www.hsa.org.uk
Soil Association: Bristol House, 40–56 Victoria Street, Bristol, BS1 6BY. Tel: 0117 314 5000. www.soilassociation.org

Glossary

Air sac Air space found at the broad end of the egg.

Baffle-boards Lengths of wood fitted under the eaves of poultry houses to prevent direct draughts but still allow ventilation.

Bean Dark, horny, triangular patch on the top of the beak of some ducks.

Blood spot Seen in the laid egg; the reasons for its appearance could be due to generic and/or nutritional causes.

Broiler Intensively reared table chicken.

Brooder Artificial heater for rearing young birds.

Broodies Hens showing an inclination to sit on their own eggs or those of another bird.

Brood spot Bare patch found on the breast of a broody hen.

Caecum One of two intestinal pouches found at the junction of the small and large intestines.

Capon Male bird which has been 'castrated' by means of a hormone injection, so that it reaches table weight more quickly.

Cloacae 'Collection' point for the bird's excrement before it is finally evacuated.

Cock Mature male after its first breeding year.

Cockerel Male bird before it is known as a cock.

Coop Small shelter, usually used to house sitting hens and/or chicks.

Coturnix Alternative name for Japanese quail.

Crop Place in which food is stored after swallowing, but before it travels through to the stomach and gizzard.

De-beaking The removal of a small portion of the top beak to prevent feather-pecking.

Dewlap Visible part of the throat or gullet often seen in breeds of geese.

Drake Male duck.

Droppings board Flat board placed below perches to collect faeces and facilitate easy access to the perches.

Duck General term but more accurately used to denote female of species.

Dummy eggs Pottery, wooden or plastic eggs used to encourage birds to lay in a certain place or to go broody.

Dust-bathing A natural way for most forms of poultry to rid themselves of lice and fleas.

Egg tooth Small 'spike' at the tip of the upper beak; it enables the chick to chip its way out of the egg and disappears several hours after hatching.

Electric energizer Unit used to supply power to electric fencing.

Feather-pecking Bad habit, which is normally caused by stress and/or overcrowding, but can, in some instances, occur for no reason at all.

Flight feathers The large primary feathers on the last half of the wing.

Fold unit Movable combined house and run.

Furnishings Removable parts of a poultry house – in other words, nest boxes, perches and so on.

Furnished Term used to describe a fully feathered bird.

Gander Male goose.

Gizzard Grinding stomach with muscular lining for pulping food.

Goose General term but more accurately used to denote female of species.

Hen Female after her first laying season.

Hover-brooders Canopies suspended from the ceiling, under which young chicks can keep warm.

Hybrid The result of crossing two or more strains, breeds or families within a breed. It will not breed true and reproduce chicks in its own likeness.

Infra-red Type of heating used for rearing chicks.

Infundibulum Funnel-shaped portion of the bird's uterine tube.

Keel Bony ridge of the breast-bone. Also, skin found hanging down from it in some ducks and geese.

Keet Guinea-fowl chick.

Keyes trays Flat fibre egg trays used for storing.

Mandible Lower or upper half of beak.

Marek's A disease causing lameness and general paralysis.

Parson's nose *See* 'Preen gland'.

Pole yard Places once commonly used to rear and fatten turkeys.

Poult Young turkey.

Pullet Young hen from hatching until the end of her first laying season.

Preen gland Oil-producing gland at the base of the rump (also known as the parson's nose).

Roach back Deformity of the vertebrae showing as a hunched back.

Saddle Either a canvas or leather 'patch' and harness used to protect female turkeys from being damaged during treading, or posterior part of back of a male bird.

Secondary feathers Quill feathers on the wing, which are usually visible when the wings are either folded or extended.

'Shooting the red' The time at which the wattles on young turkeys grow fully (about ten weeks of age).

Snood Frontal caruncle on turkeys, which is larger on the male.

Stag Male turkey.

Stubbing After plucking, the removal of new developing feathers.

Table birds Types of poultry more suited to producing meat than laying eggs.

Tassel Black 'tuft' on the chest of male turkeys.

Treading Action of male bird mating with female.

Vent Rear 'opening' through which droppings and eggs are excreted.

Wattles Folds of skin hanging from either side of the beak.

Wet plucking Traditionally preferred method of plucking for downy-feathered birds such as ducks and geese.

Index

RELATED TITLES AVAILABLE FROM CROWOOD

Bantams: Guide to Keeping, Breeding and Showing
Jeremy Hobson   ISBN 978 1 86126 786 3

The Domestic Duck
Chris and Mike Ashton   ISBN 978 1 86126 402 2

Domestic Geese
Chris Ashton   ISBN 978 1 86126 271 4

Ducks and Geese
Tom Bartlett   ISBN 978 1 85223 650 2

Exhibition Poultry Keeping
David Scrivener   ISBN 978 1 86126 739 9

Organic Farming and Growing
Francis Blake   ISBN 978 1 85223 838 4

Poultry
Carol Twinch   ISBN 978 1 85223 755 4

Poultry Farmer's & Manager's Veterinary Handbook
Peter W. Laing   ISBN 978 1 86126 261 5

Practical Poultry Keeping
David Bland   ISBN 978 1 86126 010 9

Rare Poultry Breeds
David Scrivener   ISBN 978 1 86126 889 1

The Smallholder's Manual
Katie Thear   ISBN 978 1 86126 555 5

Turkeys
David Bland   ISBN 978 1 86126 359 9

www.crowood.com